THE ART OF
CASTLE
IN THE SKY

- Possible titles
  Young Pazu and the Mystery of the Levitation Crystal, or
  Prisoner of the Castle in the Sky, or
  Flying Treasure Island, or
  The Flying Empire
- A 90-min, full-color, theatrical-release animated feature, in Vistavision
- Stereo sound

Goal of Project

If *Nausicaä of the Valley of the Wind* is a film for an older audience, then *Pazu* is targeted mainly at elementary school–age children. If *Nausicaä of the Valley of the Wind* was designed to be cool, clear, and vivid, then *Pazu* will aim to be a fun, intensely thrilling classic action film.

Pazu will be a film that young audiences can truly enjoy. *Pazu* will have laughter and tears and a sentimentally honest spirit, and will also depict themes of emotional bonding and self-sacrifice—things that modern audiences are skeptical of but, without realizing it, really crave. It will tell the story of a young boy's earnest pursuit of his dreams in an unpretentious way, in a language that modern audiences can understand.

With the exception of *Doraemon*, most current animation is based on more serious, dramatic *gekiga* comics; *Pazu* will instead aim to help resurrect traditionally entertaining manga- or cartoon-style films. By focusing mainly on an audience of fourth graders (the year when the number of cells in a child's brain reaches that of an adult), it will reach an audience of even younger children, and expand even further in its age appeal. I am certain that hundreds of thousands of older anime fans will come to see this film no matter what, so there is no need to overtly cater to their tastes. There is also a large, latent audience of older viewers who yearn for a film to enjoy with a more naïve, childlike spirit. The future of animation is threatened by the fact that for most films being planned today the target age is gradually creeping upward. More and more animated films are being made to cater to niche interests, and there is ever more subcategorization and diversification taking place. In the midst of this, it is important for us not to lose sight of the fact that animation should above all belong to children, and that truly honest works for children will also succeed with adults.

Pazu is a project to bring animation back to its roots.

Outline

Laputa is a floating island in the sky, depicted in the third part of *Gulliver's Travels*.

Formerly part of the Laputa Empire—which ruled over the nations of the earth—after the destruction of the empire, the island continued to drift through the sky. However, Laputa can also be moved at will.

Inside the island's magnificent but deserted palace, countless treasures are said to be stored—treasures stolen from the countries below.

Far off, beyond the ridges of the clouds, a fragment of a levitation crystal lands on earth, alerting people to the existence of this palace in the sky. The levitation crystal is what supported the empire of Laputa in the air, and it generates a potent force that once powered flying ships.

A man schemes to get hold of the levitation crystal, become the head of an empire in the sky, and thus lord it over the world. A girl, a descendant of ancient Laputa royalty, finds herself pursued by the man. And a boy, an apprentice mechanic who dreams of becoming an inventor, becomes entangled in the struggle over the mysterious levitation crystal.

The boy and the girl meet in the midst of great difficulties, bond with each other, and decide to help each other. But what is the true treasure that they discover hidden deep in the palace of Laputa? The story unfolds like a roller-coaster ride, with love and friendship between the boy and girl developing on one level, and an action adventure focusing on the levitation crystal and a trip to the castle in the sky taking place on another.

Story Setting

The story is set in an era when machines are still exciting and enjoyable, and science does not necessarily make people unhappy. The setting is vaguely European, but we can't tell exactly what race or nationality its people are. Humans are still masters of the world, and it still seems believable that they might change their own fates and carve their own ways in life.

Peace reigns in the bountiful land; farmers take joy in their harvests, craftsmen take pride in their work, and merchants take good care of the goods they sell. There is no conflict between the townspeople and the farmers, and a gentle equilibrium reigns. People are responsible for their own styles of living. There are some poor people, but they help each other. Sometimes the harvests are rich, sometimes there are droughts and famines. It is a world where bad people coexist with good people, but bad people are easily identifiable from the way they look.

In terms of visuals, we will fully use our imaginations and create a world that, while fictional, has a real sense of presence. The machines in this world are not the products of mass production, rather they still possess the inherent warmth of handcrafted things. There are no electric lights; illumination is provided by either candles or gaslights. Instead of pipes with running water, people use abundant wells or springs. The vehicles in this world are a diverse collection of hand-built, eccentric inventions. One example of this is the ornithopter, a flying machine with flapping wings that the hero Pazu rides around on. It functions similarly to the *mehve* in Nausicaä. and becomes an important character in its own right. The vehicles, weapons, and hideouts used by the bad guys in this story are also a collection of eccentric inventions, and the harmonious atmosphere they create, along with the setting itself, will make the world of this film even more enjoyable.

Hayao Miyazaki
December 7, 1984

"Boy Playing Trumpet," drawn for the title page of *Hayao Miyazaki Concept Art Collection* (Kodansha). This image was originally created for another project, but it ended up being used as the concept for Pazu in *Castle in the Sky.*

The proposal for *Castle in the Sky* first came from director Hayao Miyazaki on December 7, 1984, nine months after the release of *Nausicaä of the Valley of the Wind*. This moment should be the natural starting point for this essay, but when I look back on that time now, I feel that the various states of confusion I was privileged to witness in Mr. Miyazaki during the events of those nine months—mainly the reaction toward *Nausicaä*—make this a deeply interesting period, one of the artist struggling toward his next work. So it is with this time, then, that I would like to start.

1.

In March 1984, after the release of *Nausicaä of the Valley of the Wind* (which actually exceeded all expectations to do very well), Mr. Miyazaki accepted an invitation to an anime convention in Kyushu and was on his way to Hakata a few days later after having sat in the studio for nearly a year. Naturally, at this time, he was feeling carefree and intent on simply letting his mind wander.

"That place Yanagawa's not that far away. Let's go take a peek while we're here."

This casual suggestion was interesting because it ended up being a clue toward the structure of projects to come later.

"Is there anything there? Like Yanagawa *nabe* stew or something?" asked the Animage Editorial Division editor accompanying him.
"Come on, it's a beautiful riverside area, the home of Hakushu Kitahara."
"Oh, now that you mention it, Kazuo Dan's…"

And so, they turned Mr. Miyazaki's beloved Citroën 2CV toward the small city on the Ariake Sea. Here, they ate *unagi* before getting on a ferry headed downstream along a waterway around the area. The editor enjoyed the food, and Mr. Miyazaki felt that the view, befitting as it was for a city on the water, eased his fatigue.

And yet, even as he allowed his mind to wander and take this view in, swirling around in the back of Mr. Miyazaki's brain was still *Nausicaä*, which he had in fact been furiously at work on only a month before.

"I thought it might end up being one of those movies people either love or hate, and I guess it is."

Every so often, a thought like this would pop out of him, as if he were only just recalling it. A mountain of letters containing a mountain of opinions had already arrived at the editorial division, letters which Mr. Miyazaki had looked over. Of course, there were far and away more people writing to say that they loved it; many had been captivated by a certain wonderful scene. Mr. Miyazaki counted these among the ones who didn't "understand" the film.

"When you have a box-office hit, talk of a sequel does come up, doesn't it?"
"…."

The look on Mr. Miyazaki's face often grew complicated when anyone mentioned this. He had made *Nausicaä* and was now feeling strong pressure from

two sides. He himself discusses one of these sides in *Nausicaä Roman Album*:

"I had no intention of making her (Nausicaä) a Joan of Arc, and even though I tried to remove any religious coloring, you get to the end, and it turns into a religious painting (Nausicaä is raised up by Ohm, the sky dyed golden with the morning light)."

Initially, he planned to have the Ohm physically stop in front of Nausicaä, but during the storyboard process, he ended up not having them stop, a revelation of sorts that was very confusing to the man himself.

Given that some people were giving his film ten out of ten because of this moment, he felt he had stepped into unexpected territory, a thought that weighed heavily on his heart.

The other pressure he faced was that there were "a lot of elementary school children" among the moviegoers he saw when he went to introduce the film on the day of its release (at three theaters). This despite the fact that the first day is normally packed with rabid fans (Miyazaki fans are relatively older). Apparently, he thought he'd whiffed it.

The idea that it might be all right to go along as he had been and make animation an adult thing also connects with *Castle in the Sky*, but I'm getting a little ahead of myself.

"The other day, I got an invitation from a religious group."
"Are you going?"
"I'm not going, but it did make me think that I created something unexpected here."

They got off the ferry and started walking from Hakushu's house in the direction that smelled like the ocean. Suddenly, without any warning whatsoever, a boat mast sprang up from amidst the row of houses. The difference between high and low tides in the Ariake Sea is the greatest in Japan, and several dozen boats had been pulled in from the waves flowing along the river edge. Our eyes were unconsciously drawn to the strange sight of town and port connected without any real border.

The fishing district spread out on both coasts among the herds of boats. In the laziness of the almost soundless afternoon, tanned children were playing at building houses with scraps of wood.

"The fish seller before was strange, hm?"

An innocent excitement came over the editor, who loved fish, as he remembered the fish seller and the boxes of Ise shrimp and shellfish and things he'd never seen before all crammed together, while next to him Mr. Miyazaki ignored him, caught up in a particular insight.

"A place like this—population of tens of thousands, tourist spots and the fishing district right there, right next to each other—Yanagawa could be the setting for a coming-of-age story."

And this is the difference between a first-rate storyteller, always looking for something more, and a simple fish lover looking at the same scene.

2.

After the holiday in Yanagawa was over, this proposal of Miyazaki's—provisionally called *Blue Mountains* in the initial proposal by then-*Animage* Editor-in-Chief Hideo Ogata, because we'd run into trouble without some kind of title—surfaced in reality once Mr. Miyazaki opened an office in Asagaya, Tokyo, christened "Nibariki" (not "Nibaka," which, of course, means "two idiots") in the middle of April.

Entertainment-wise, *Nausicaä* was a success, and quite naturally, Tokuma Shoten had asked Mr. Miyazaki to give them a plan for his next projects, including *Nausicaä Part 2*.

"Could you maybe do that?"

Mr. Miyazaki responded to this request with the project concept of a coming-of-age story depicting the experience of female cousins who come from Tokyo to Yanagawa for a summer. That initial idea in Yanagawa had grown in the head of this natural storyteller.

At the beginning of May, it was decided that this proposal would go to director Isao Takahata. Mr. Miyazaki was put on design and layout. The plan on paper was that they would have pictures drawn with the help of other main staff members and put together a studio by the beginning of the fall. (In the end, this planning on paper for *Blue Mountains* proved to be considerably useful when we got to *Castle in the Sky*.)

Anyway, the details. It was an extremely difficult coming-of-age story, one that would make you feel good if it got made, a coming-of-age story that would have a real impact on pretty much everyone, but also vivid enough that viewers would remember and find their own young selves in the characters onscreen.

What were the requirements for *Blue Mountains*?

• Characters reflecting the time period
• Aiming to be a hit in the entertainment industry
• Breakdown of various real-world problems
• High school student protagonist incorporating broader social issues as well as problems at school and home

This was the general idea behind Mr. Takahata and Mr. Miyazaki's story, but developing any or all of these in detail would lead to nothing but headaches. And indeed, Mr. Miyazaki's story building ran aground any number of times.

In the beginning, a high school girl running along a canal. *Tak tak tak!* Or it starts with a boy riding his bicycle and falling into the canal. At any rate, the two meet. The girl lives in a fishing village, a *beautiful girl* (!) who catches clams as a part-time job.

And just as he thought, *Mm, that's a promising start*, he was faced with the struggle of where to go with the broader social issue.

How about a hidden canal? The place is a city now, but if you look at it from a certain bridge at a certain angle, you can tell that there used to be a canal over there. That canal, disappearing as the city grew; where did it start, where did it end? A group of boys begin to investigate and stumble into the secret of the beautiful girl's birth, and things move in an unexpected direction.

The issue of water and people is an eternal theme, and at that time, the newspapers and other media were reporting on the symposium being held on pollution in Lake Biwa, so it was also timely.

"And now that I'm thinking about it, there was also the Yanagawa culvert thing a few years back too," noted Susumu Kubo, Nibariki administrative director (although there was only just him to administrate). Put a lid on a canal that's now a ditch and increase the use value by making it a parking lot or something; it's a city plan that could happen anywhere in Japan. Whenever this sort of thing is proposed, a section chief from city hall investigates the historical role and what have you of the canal, and offers a counterproposal to instead clean it up and use it. Apparently, in Yanagawa, this proposal had passed, and the waters were restored.

Mr. Takahata still hadn't seen the city. With the idea he should go to the site once at any rate, he went to Yanagawa in the middle of June with Susumu Kubo.

During this time, as we read the British children's books (which are extremely interesting, and if you have some time, I would recommend you pick one up—you'll find another very clear starting point for Mr. Miyazaki that's not science fiction or action) in the "topic library" put forth by Mr. Miyazaki, like *Pirate's Island*, *Minnow on the Say*, and *Colonel Sheperton's Clock*, we also moved forward on the creation of the studio.

Studio Kesennuma, Musashino Video, Studio Kame, etc., etc. The name didn't matter; our orders were to find a studio with big windows and a single floor on the outside of Ring Road 8. Eventually, we gave it the name Ghibli— a World War I Italian fighter plane and a hot wind that blows in Africa—which was only registered in June.

We made steady progress building our environment, and Mr. Takahata returned to Tokyo on June 18, arms full of research materials. He went to discuss everything with Mr. Miyazaki right away. The tentative title *The City of Flowing Water* was put forth a few days later, and we were told the story would be written by the end of June, giving us the impression that our work was basically done, but things never go quite as smoothly as we expect.

The Yanagawa culvert incident of eight years earlier that Mr. Takahata had been investigating was just too heavy to bring into the story.

There is no greater wealth than having a good relationship with water. However, all over Japan, the environment suffered as the country modernized and urbanized; there was no doubt that people were the ones behind this destruction. But why did that not happen in Yanagawa? It goes without saying the city hall section chief—Tsutae Hiromatsu—put up a good fight, but wasn't there something deeper, something innately connected to, for instance, human existence?

Immediately understanding that Mr. Takahata's interest lay somewhere other than the planned film, Mr. Miyazaki felt that this would likely be the perfect subject for a documentary film. Perhaps also intending it as a thank-you for accepting the role of producer on *Nausicaä*, he proposed that Mr. Takahata make the film using all the revenue Nibariki had earned from *Nausicaä* if he needed to.

Mr. Takahata agreed enthusiastically, so *Blue Mountains* eventually changed shape into the cultural documentary *Town Around Water: The Story of Yanagawa's Canals*. (Just over two years have passed, and as of the present—October 1986—the editing is finished, and the film looks to be completed this year. I've seen the rushes, and although it looks subdued, it seems like it will be an extremely interesting film. I do hope you'll find the chance to watch.)

And of plans for films which disappeared never to actually be seen, there are no doubt a fair number like this, live-action films included, so it's really just a matter of luck which films make it to the theater, whether they're a hit or not. In the case of this coming-of-age story, it leaves behind this documentary film on the same level of excellence, so it clearly falls into the lucky category.

3.

I've used a few too many pages in my desire to convey just how very difficult the birth pangs can be. Let's hurry ahead.

As these birth pangs continued through into December of this year, we had four projects, if we only count the main plans Mr. Miyazaki put forward: *My Neighbor Totoro*, *Princess Mononoke*, a warring states story, and *Tales from Earthsea*.

Each one of these was carefully discussed, albeit not quite on the level of the coming-of-age story. To skip to the end, it was decided that getting the rights to make Ursula K. Le Guin's *Earthsea* was too difficult. *Princess Mononoke* would have been hard to turn into the hit Tokuma Shoten wanted. *My Neighbor Totoro* was a bit mellow, with its boy and girl protagonists simply living their lives against a vibrant background of still-poor Japan in the 1940s, but this was also a work that would likely be warmly welcomed now, in a modern Japan looking toward its beginnings forty years after the war. For the warring states story, we were sure to have a terrible time trying to find animators who could make a horse run properly. (That said, it's not as if they don't exist, so enough to leave this to rise to the top if the opportunity arises.)

And *Totoro* doesn't necessarily follow so directly or clearly from *Nausicaä*. Opinions were divided on whether it was better to have something that followed more directly or if fans wanted to see something more different. Our worries were Mr. Miyazaki's worries; this was a time of upheaval for all of us.

"Paku (Takahata) took up that documentary film, which tackles some of the themes of *Nausicaä*, so I can relax about that. I want to try and make

Treasure Island (in the sense of an adventure story with girls and boys) or something."

Now that I'm thinking about it, we were talking about this sort of thing long before the name Laputa ever came up.

At any rate, I really can't remember what led to deciding on *Castle in the Sky* in the end. I will have to ask the reader to infer that from everything I've related thus far.

On the afternoon of December 7, we in the Animage Editorial Division received a sudden call from Mr. Miyazaki. We hurried over to Nibariki to find that he had, in fact, finished the proposal for *Castle in the Sky*.

4.

The intention behind the plan was dazzling, and we were fascinated at being able to see the preparation that was the result of Mr. Miyazaki's struggles.

"If *Nausicaä of the Valley of the Wind* targeted an older demographic, then *Pazu*'s central target is elementary school students. If we were aiming for a cool, clear, striking work with *Nausicaä*, then with *Pazu*, we're aiming for an old-school action movie to make your blood sing.
What *Pazu* is trying to be is a movie to first soothe the hearts of young viewers, a spectacle they can enjoy and delight in. Laughter and tears, an honest heart overflowing with real feeling—things that are currently avoided at all costs. Even if viewers don't actually realize it, this work describes in words through today's viewers the ideal of a young boy moving forward earnestly toward something he believes in—the meeting of hearts, contribution to a partner, friendship—without being caught up in it."

The boy and girl adventure/action movie that was Mr. Miyazaki's initial aim was also very clearly on display in the tentative titles given in the proposal:

The Boy Pazu: The Mystery of the Etherium Crystal
The Boy Pazu: Captive of the Castle in the Sky
The Boy Pazu: Flying Treasure Island
The Boy Pazu: The Flying Kingdom

The assumed running time was ninety minutes. "A primitive adventure story's possible in ninety minutes," Mr. Miyazaki would remark almost daily.

And the details too showed nothing more than the skeleton of a very old-school adventure story just as the man himself had said, from the elements of the hero and heroine, the villain (this was simply a man who aspired to become king of the flying kingdom and rule the world), a treasure island (the flying kingdom), and a small tool (the etherium crystal).

"This is exactly the sort of plan I always want to see from you. But in this day and age, establishing a 'treasure island' is next to impossible." Mr. Isao Takahata, once again assigned the role of producer, could predict with terrifying insight, even at this stage, the double and triple structure of *Castle in the Sky*—that it would not end with a simple "treasure island."

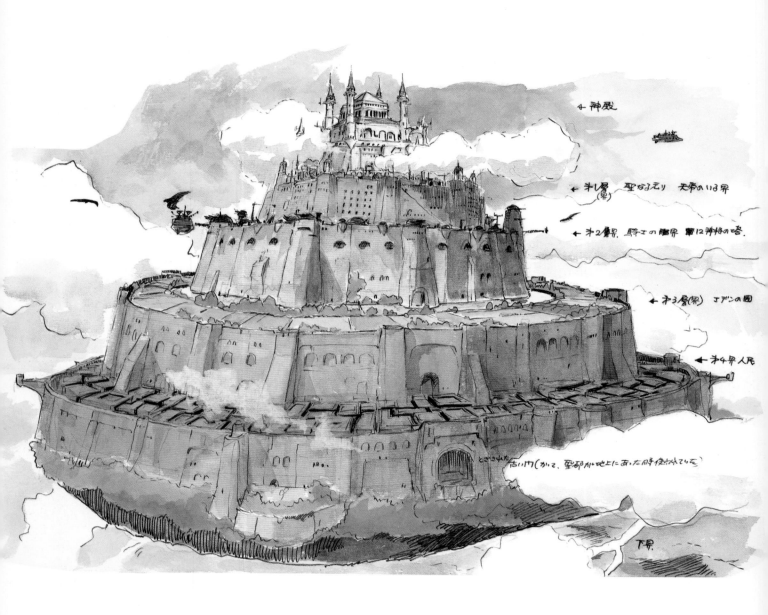

→ 神殿

← 第1層 聖なるエリ 天帝のいる界
（界）

← 第2層界、騎士の騎界 都に神将の塔.

← 第3層(界) Jアデンの園

← 第4界 人民

古い門（かつて、聖部が地上にあった時使われていた）

下界.

Concept sketch for the castle in the sky, drawn before the *Castle in the Sky* plan. The concept was that the castle was divided into four levels, with the class of the people depending on what level they lived in.

At the beginning of 1985, in February, the manga serialization of *Nausicaä* was put on hold for a month, and Mr. Miyazaki got down to the business of putting some flesh on this skeleton.

At the end of February, the second draft of the plan was finished.

The biggest element not in the first draft was the "artificial human (robot) made with extremely advanced science and technology" and a military leader with eyes on Laputa and its lode of modern weapons.

Eventually, another set of protagonists popped their heads up in the form of the pirates, the Dola clan.

The most important change was that the castle, the treasure island where vast fortunes slept in the first draft, actually had another side as an enormous military base.

At this time, there was nothing for us to do. We could only watch as the work changed shape in the hands of the author, like a magic trick, and became more and more fleshed out and more and more interesting.

May 1985. Location scouting for two weeks in Wales, Great Britain.

"The scenery there was different from Miya's stock up to that point. Unlike the slopes and rocky mountains of Switzerland or Italy, there are no tall mountains in England; there are just places in every region people had a hand in. The trees had all been planted." This according to a proposal from Mr. Takahata. But had this been the case for the period background of the time of the Industrial Revolution? (The stock up to now has been Italy and Argentina for *Three Thousand Leagues*, Sweden for *Pippi*, Switzerland and Germany for *Heidi*, among others.)

I heard they went round coal mines, castles, museums (there are many museums in England aiming at dynamic preservation; some do performances using the tools of the Industrial Revolution) and learned a great many things. These are strongly reflected in Slag Ravine where Pazu lives, the scenery, and the castle.

June 15. Ghibli, the studio, opens.

July 1. First draft of the script completed. (Second draft completed around July 15.)

In the second draft of the proposal and the script, the nature of the castle shifts even further. In the middle of June, Mr. Miyazaki also started work on the concept art while writing the script, but the concept art for *Castle in the Sky* drawn between July 1 and 23 has a green canopy not seen in the pages before that.

The castle, with the two aspects of treasure island and military base, became a storehouse of natural riches as well. Accompanying this, Sheeta's stone went from the initial, simple etherium crystal to a stone demonstrating power when hit with the light of the moon (in the plan's second draft), and in the script stage, the idea was that

it responded to Sheeta's thoughts. It was also the source of Laputa's thunder energy and possessed a power that could be said to be the root of the life force, making buds sprout from the stumps of trees.

If this had been thirty years earlier, if it had been the era when humanity had still not climbed the tallest mountain on Earth, when it was written in encyclopedias that if one went further into Tibet, there might be a mountain far taller than Everest, when Africa was called the "Dark Continent," the story might have found form as an old adventure from that time. For children of that era, "treasure island" symbolized these things unconditionally.

Thanking us for our work in completing the script, Mr. Miyazaki showed us a momentary sadness. "I've long thought I wanted to make an old-school adventure story, but the era we're in now, it's no longer possible." And then, "Okay, let's do it!" he raised his voice, dominating the entire studio, before throwing himself into the storyboard before him.

*   *

May 14, 1985:	The final production budget proposal for *Castle in the Sky* is complete.
May 18:	Director Miyazaki location scouting in Wales for two weeks.
June 15:	Opening of Studio Ghibli (253 m², with elevator).
June 17:	Director Miyazaki joins studio.
July 1:	Director Miyazaki's first script draft complete.
July 18:	Art Director Toshiro Nozaki joins studio.
July 22:	Second draft of script printed.
August 5:	Animation Director Tsukasa Tannai joins studio.
August 16:	Chief Animator Yoshinori Kaneda join studio. Creates flaptor flight motion test in August.
End of August:	Part A of Director Miyazaki's storyboard (401 shots) complete.
September 5:	First music meeting.
September 6:	Art Director Nizo Yamamoto joins studio.
September 19:	Title logo complete for *Castle in the Sky*.
September 24:	First part of *Animage* serialization of the novel *Castle in the Sky* complete.
End of September:	Ten animators join the studio. Flaptor flight motion test redone. Storyboard part B completed (total of 1,002 shots for A and B).

October 6:	Six background artists join studio.
October 9:	Director Miyazaki talks about a theatrical animation proposal *Totsugeki Aianpoku!* (70 minutes).
October 17:	*Castle in the Sky* press conference (location: Tokyo Akasaka Prince Hotel).
October 21:	Conversation between Hideo Takayama (head of Children's Research Center) and Hayao Miyazaki (location: Studio Ghibli).
October 31:	*Castle in the Sky* kickoff party, approximately eighty related personnel attend (location: Kichijoji Tokyu Inn).
End of October:	Total of twenty animators join the studio.
End of November:	Total of thirty animators join the studio. Storyboard with a total of 1,107 shots complete.
December 11:	New Year's holiday theatrical *Castle in the Sky* teaser complete.
December 13:	Conversation between Baku Yumemakura and Hayao Miyazaki (location: Studio Ghibli).
December 30:	End of work at Studio Ghibli.
January 4, 1986:	Start of work at Studio Ghibli.
End of January:	Total of thirty-three animators join the studio. Storyboard of 1,360 shots complete.
Beginning of February:	Shooting starts (Takahashi Productions).
February 5:	Joe Hisaishi decided on for music.
February 10:	Proposal for screening with *Sherlock Hound.*
February 13:	Conversation between Tsuneya Ohno (Professor, Bacteriology Center No. 1, Jikei University School of Medicine) and Hayao Miyazaki (location: Studio Ghibli).
February 25:	Spring holiday theatrical teaser complete.
End of February:	Storyboard complete. Total of 1,657 shots.
March 4:	Image song "The Girl Who Fell from the Sky" (Joe Hisaishi. Released by Tokuma Japan) recorded.
March 5:	Image song "Moshimo Sora o Tobetara" ordered from Takahashi Matsumoto (lyrics) and Kyohei Tsutsumi (composition) (sung by Yoko Obata).
March 10:	Screening with *Continuing with Sherlock Hound* decided. (Other proposals include *Sherlock Hound: Three Dangerous Blows* and *The Game's Afoot, Sherlock Hound!*)
March 26, 29:	Music meetings with Joe Hisaishi (location: Studio Ghibli).
May 23:	Audio Director Shigeharu Shiba first casting meeting (location: Studio Ghibli).
May 25:	Image songs released.
June 10:	Meeting for selection of singer for soundtrack song "Carrying You."
June 20:	All rush print (location: Kichijoji Toei).
June 28:	Postrecording (location: Tokyo TV Center; mainly scenes featuring just Pazu and Sheeta.)
July 5–6:	Postrecording.
July 14–17:	Dubbing (location: Tokyo TV Center).
July 20:	*Castle in the Sky* fan event (location: Shibuya Pantheon).
July 21:	Test screening (location: Imagica).
July 23:	First screening.
July 25:	Complete screening event (location: Tokyo Chamber of Commerce Hall).
July 29:	*Yushu Eiga Kanshokai* (Excellent Film Appreciation Society) recommended movie.
July 30:	*Seishonen Eiga Shingikai* (Youth Film Committee) selection.
August 2:	Nationwide release as Western-style film.
August 14:	*Chuo Jido Fukushi Shingikai Suisen Bunkazai* (Central Committee for Children's Welfare Cultural Asset) special recommendation.

- Total number of shots (including OP, ED): 1,664. Total length: 124 minutes, 4 seconds, 22 frames. Number of cels used: 75,000.
- Viewer survey results (Toei, survey date August 2)
- Average age: 19; Male: 62.4%; Female: 37.6%; Satisfaction level: 97.7% (Reference: *Nausicaä of the Valley of the Wind* 97.7%).

—Osamu Kameyama, Animage Editorial Division

Concept sketch of Pazu and Sheeta, *Castle in the Sky* protagonists, from
when Sheeta was thought to be the daughter of pirates.

This collection is made up of concept art, cels, film, and concept sketches for the animated film *Castle in the Sky* created, written, and directed by Hayao Miyazaki.

All concept sketches, initial designs, and character notes are by Hayao Miyazaki, and comments in the text are taken from interviews with Hayao Miyazaki.

Additionally, the technical explanations in the text were written with the kind assistance of production assistant Tsutomu Iida (Oh! Pro Office).

Image processing and backgrounds were not done for some cels, and there may be some that differ from the original art.

THE ART OF
CASTLE
IN THE SKY

The beginning of the story, unseen in the film.

PROLOGUE

4

5

6

7

1–6 The film starts with Dola's aerial attack, but the story
leading up to that moment was written as a novel for the
monthly *Animage*. These six illustrations were drawn for the
serialization of that novel.
7 Frontispiece illustration for the first installment of the
novel serialization (all printed in two colors at the time of
release).

1

2

1–3, 5–7 Beginning of the film. [Concept sketches]
    "The beginning's very important for a film. Which is why, rather than do it as a storyboard, I drew this succession of images to really get a solid hold on the concept. However, a lot of them do overlap with the design images."
4   *Tiger Moth* flying in a sea of clouds. [Film]

3

4

5

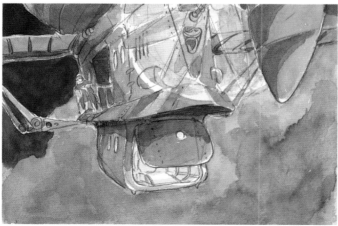

6

7

1–2 Beginning of the film. [Concept sketches]
3 Sheeta staring out the window of a room in the airship. [Film]
4 Sheeta inside the room. [Novel illustration]
5 Flaptors approaching the airship. [Film]
6 Flaptors firing accelerating rockets. [Film]

1

3

2

4

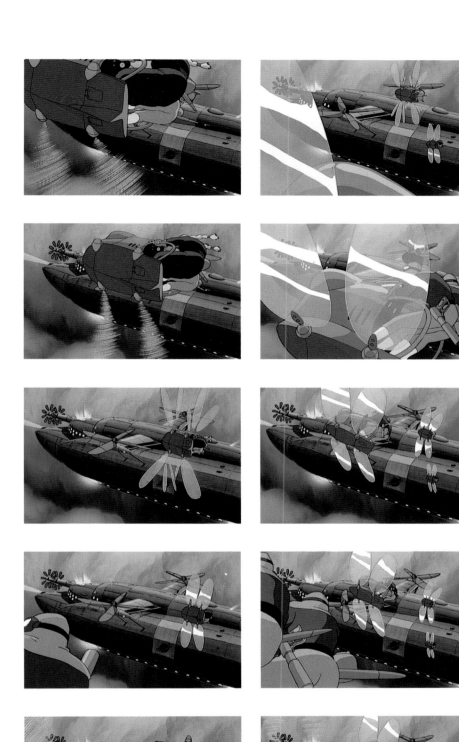
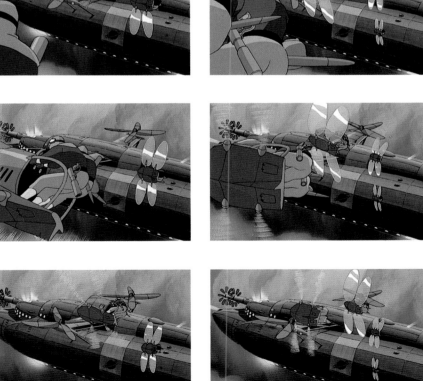

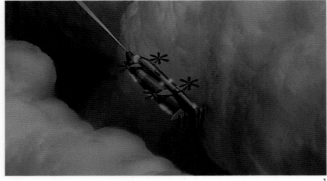

1

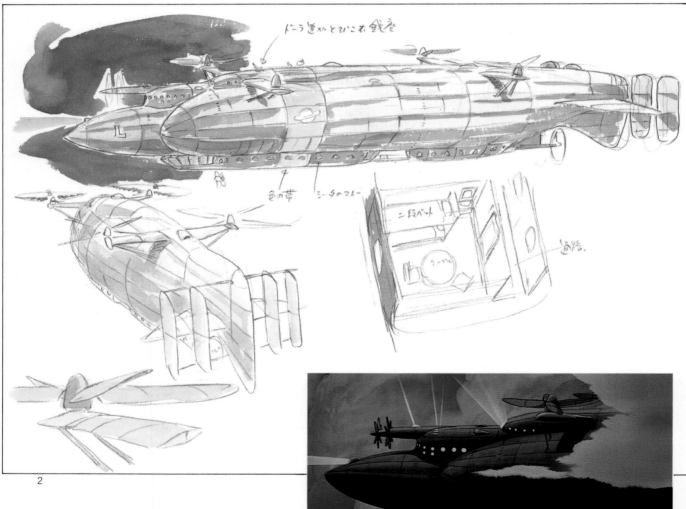

2

3

1, 3　Airship flying through sea of clouds. [Film]
2　　Initial airship design.
4　　Airship. [Concept sketch]
　　　"At first, I thought that a military transport ship
　　　would carry Sheeta, but I decided to make Muska a
　　　civilian and have them ride in a normal passenger
　　　ship. The ship has the mark of Saturn on it, so I
　　　suppose it could be called the *Saturn*, hm? Because
　　　Saturn used to be quite mysterious. And each time
　　　I drew this ship, it changed on me, which gave me a
　　　bit of trouble."
5–6　Airship cockpit.
　　　"So the GZA, writing Z makes it like the name of
　　　an airship in German, so I tried putting a G before
　　　that. It basically means there's gas inside, perhaps.
　　　[*laughs*]"
7　　Airship cockpit. [Film]
8　　Airship salon. [Film]

4

5

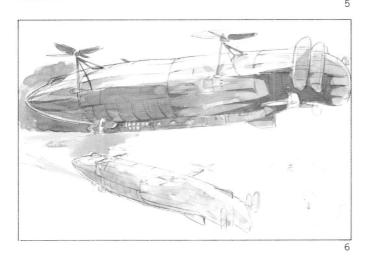

6

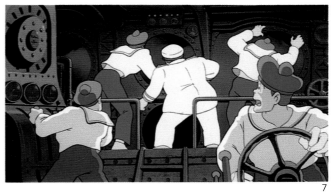

7

8

1

2

3

4

1–2, 4–5 Beginning of the film. [Concept sketches]

"I drew both the regular airship and *Goliath*, thinking of the rigid airship as a base, the so-called zeppelin, and it is true that the airship's control room is below the balloon part. But I thought having it below would make it too hard for Dola and her group to get in, so I put the cockpit on top."

3 Dola shooting a gun. [Film]

"This gun is for the purpose of threatening. I was thinking of mustard gas canisters."

5

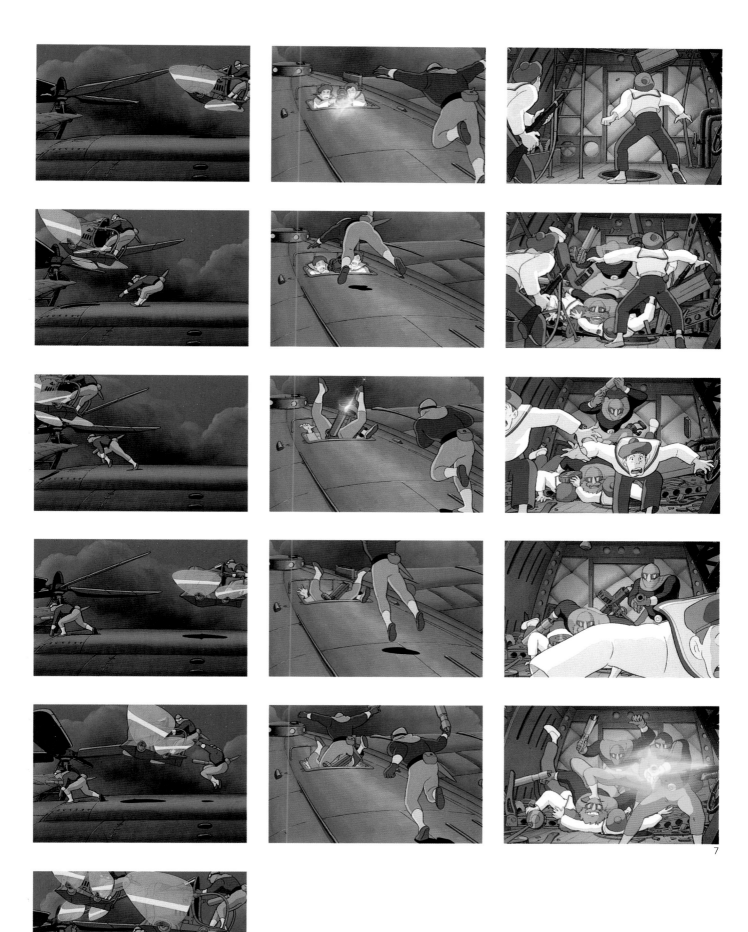

6   Dola family transferring to the airship. [Film]
7   Dola family invading the airship. [Film]
     "I wanted to make the pirates seem like they were proud of not killing people.
     They have a blinding gun and fisticuffs, that's about it."

6

1   Muska tapping on the telegraph key of the wireless. [Cel]

2, 4–6 Sheeta in the room. [Cel]

3   Sheeta putting on the etherium crystal. [Film]

7–10 Sheeta fleeing the pirates. [Concept sketch]
"I thought about having Sheeta run away using the structure of the passenger ship, but dawdling along right before the title sequence wouldn't do. She's going to fall anyway, so I ended up just having her go on and fall. [*laughs*]"

1

2

3

4

5

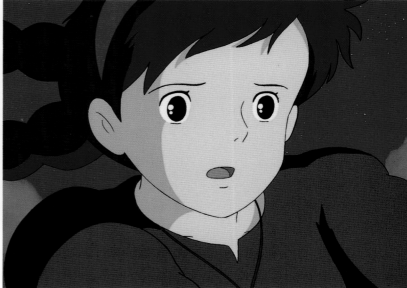

6

7

8

9

10

1

2

3

4

5

6

7

1   Opening title. [Film]
2, 6–7, 15–27 Opening title. [Cel]
3–5, 8–14 Opening title. [Concept sketch]
    "So this goes from being a windmill that turns in
    the wind to one that turns even without wind and
    continues into a propeller. With it spinning around
    like that, you also get the notion of an engine."

8

9

10

11

15

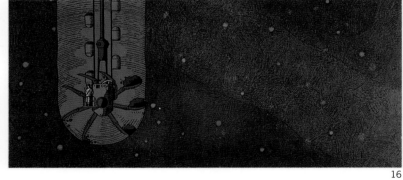

16

17

18

12

13

19

14

20

23

25

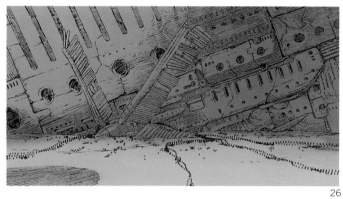

24

26

27

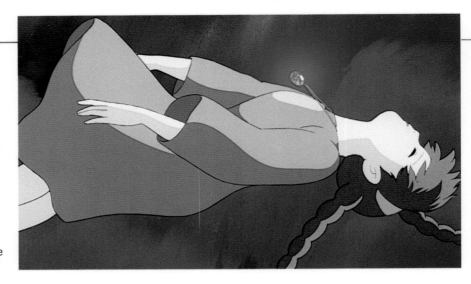

Sheeta falling from the airship. However, the power hidden in the etherium crystal saves her.

Three types of transmitted light and lith film work

This shot, where the etherium crystal reacts to Sheeta's fall and magically (?!) stabilizes her movement, incorporates all three kinds of transmitted light elements used in *Castle in the Sky*: transmitted light, colored transmitted light, and special transmitted light.

1. Transmitted light: First, Sheeta and the background sky are filmed without the transmitted light. The film is wound back and only the transmitted light is double-exposed. This is why Sheeta shows through under the transmitted light.

The first time this is done, it can very easily affect the film material; if the material is bright, the colors and light end up washed out. The amount of transmitted light can be increased to avoid this, but then the structure becomes indefinite because of flare, which is a weak point of this method.

2. Colored transmitted light: This is a special technique devised to overcome transmitted light's weak point. The transmitted light area is blackened, just like in the first pass at filming. This allows the transmitted light to spread well. But this method also has a weak point. In addition to the concave mask of transmitted light, you also need a convex black mask, so the work is doubled.

3. Special transmitted light: This is basically the same as colored transmitted light, but now the work is done with the light source itself when filming the second time. The film is lit indirectly with Christmas tinsel beneath the filming platform to make the light shimmer. The amount of transmitted light for the colored transmitted light on the etherium crystal was quite restricted to bring out the color more beautifully, so it's on the darker side. Because of this, the flare (the light bleeding out around the transmitted light) is smaller, and the very slight mask slippage becomes a black shadow on the screen. Normally, the part to be given transmitted light, which is noted in pencil in the video, is copied to two cels; in one, only the area for transmitted light is colored black and everything else is colored normally, while in the other cel, the part receiving transmitted light is cut out with everything else being colored black. You can't use male/female masks with this method.

The outline of the etherium crystal was copied from the film onto the cel using a xerography machine, so male and female would both be the same black line, but with colored transmitted light and its almost total lack of flare, this line doesn't disappear and shows up clearly in the image.

And this is where lith film comes in. Lith film is like the negative of a photograph and is fairly useful in that the part drawn in black on the cel is cut out and the white parts come out black.

So let's take a look at what materials were prepared to actually film this shot.
Cel A: Moonlight-colored Sheeta.
Cel A': Etherium crystal-colored Sheeta, exactly the same picture as Cel A.
Cel B: Etherium crystal reflection.
Cel C: Etherium crystal itself, normal coloring.
Cel C': Etherium crystal itself, black coloring.
Cel C": Etherium crystal itself, transmitted light mask.
Cel D: Etherium crystal emblem area.
Cel F: Black colored shadow for double exposure shadow.
Cel F': Transmitted light mask for light beam No. 1.
Cel G: Female mask for light beam No. 2.
Cel G': Transmission mask for light beam No. 2.

Sheeta colored by moonlight and falling. Layer cels A, B, and D, slide over the background in response to the filming, while for the etherium crystal, cels C and C' are overlapping (O/L), to make colored transmitted light, and the transmitted light of cel C" is set to fade in (F/I).

The etherium crystal releases its power, and beams of light come gushing out. The beams of light are created with the transmitted light of the masks of cels F, G, and G'. This is set to F/O with the aim of making the emblem of cel D no longer visible due to the beams of light. Additionally, until this point, the light source was the moonlight, but it now changes to the etherium crystal, so cels A and A' are O/L, and Sheeta's color changes. Cel E adds variation to the image as the light shadow (?!) with a double exposure.

Then the etherium crystal enters a state of stabilized motion. This is expressed through Cel A', changed with O/L, and the special transmitted light cels C' and C".

1

2

4

3

1, 4　Mine town at night. [Background]
2, 3　Mine town. [Concept sketch]
　"I was drawing the streets of the town even before we went on the research trip to Wales. I think this is one of those. I also did *Sherlock Hound* before, so thanks to that, I had already done some research on houses and things in England.

　"The store where Pazu buys supper has a hearth outside, and there was actually a shop like this when we went on the trip to China. I thought then that I would use it in a project someday."

4

5

6

1, 3   The mine where Pazu works. [Background]

2   Inside the mine. [Concept art]

4   Slag Ravine. [Concept sketch]

"I drew this before I had decided where Sheeta was going to fall. I had the idea of them digging out a mine that's already been dug out once, and I figured they'd put a steam engine in the hole. I considered several different things for the part where Sheeta falls, like making it on top of Pazu's hut or having him find her hanging from a tree in the morning. And then I thought I'd just get straight to the point and have her fall at Pazu's workplace.

"But I had the idea of rather than her simply falling onto the ground, she'd fall into the hole, so you wouldn't know how far she might end up going. And then I realized that there needed to be a place in the hole where Pazu could catch Sheeta, so I added the steam engine hoist."

5, 6   With the boss and the steam engine. [Film]

1, 2, 7 Pazu catching Sheeta. [Film and cel]
3–5 Sheeta falling. [Concept sketch]
"When I drew these, I hadn't decided where she
would fall."
6 Sheeta in Pazu's arms. [Film]
8 Sheeta unconscious. [Cel]

6

7

パズー

2

パズー

1–3　Pazu. [Design]
"I drew these back when I was
thinking about the kind of children
Pazu and Sheeta would be."

3

4   Pazu apprentice pirate. [Concept sketch]
    "This is one of the pages I drew when I
    was thinking he might dress like a pirate
    when he's caught by them or what he'd
    be like if he were a pirate boy."

5   Pazu's tool bag. [Design]
    "Rather than making Pazu some cool kid,
    I thought he would work better as a boy
    who'd yank all kinds of tools from his bag
    and get to work. So I drew a lot of things
    for the bag, but they wouldn't actually all fit
    inside. [laughs] And how did he get those
    fried eggs in there too? [laughs]"

シータ・トエル・熱・ラピ°2タ
            りル

1–2, 7 Sheeta. [Design]

"I took Sheeta's name from the θ (theta) in Mathematics. I thought it was kind of a strange character. A queen by the name of Sita also appears in the *Ramayana*, but for me, it's the Greek letter θ. What I took particular care with this time were her pupils. I had the idea of something slightly manga-like, so I was thinking about taking away any adornments and making them black like in the old days. If I made her eyes the more fashionable glass-like eyes, you wouldn't be able to tell what she was looking at. When we did *Flying Phantom Ship*, that sort of eye was used in close-ups, but you can't tell where the eyes are looking. Ever since then, I've made a conscious choice not to use white pupils. With this project, it varied with the shot, but there are some with pupils. I think now it would've been better if I had made them all black."

3–6 Sheeta. [Initial design]

"I drew a fair number of pictures of Sheeta, although just one would've been fine. As I worked on them, I lost the sense of her presence as a character in a movie. I ended up really wanting her body to be solidly built when we moved her as a character.

"Her head and her shoulders are about the same width. This is no good.

"Because there's the part with Sheeta falling from the sky, I thought something sensual would be better than a light-looking little girl. [*laughs*] Although there are parts where she's a little too heavy. I did this one talking with the animation director Tannai, when we discussed how if her ankles were going to be thin, then it would be okay if her thighs were heavier. I didn't notice this when I was drawing, but I often wondered why they make them so thin in things like *Conan, the Boy in Future*.

"Because in animation, what's more important than whether a single drawing is good or not is how it moves."

4

5

シータ(B等)

シータ.
ラプタの遣に

46

6

1   *Tiger Moth* floating in the air. [Cel]

"The name of the airship is *Tiger Moth*. But if you were to ask if the tiger moth has anything to do with it, not really. I just used it because I liked the name.

"When I came up with *Tiger Moth*, I was basically thinking of something that was not airtight. The idea was that you'd be able to tell pretty clearly what someone was doing and where. The whole thing would lack a certain flavor if they were all just running around inside the ship. And when I thought about it, this is what I ended up with.

"Although this form does completely ignore air resistance. [*laughs*]"

2–3   *Tiger Moth* and the flaptor aircraft based in it. [Cel]

4–5   *Tiger Moth* and flaptors. [Film]

1

2

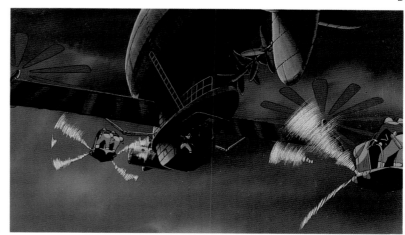

3

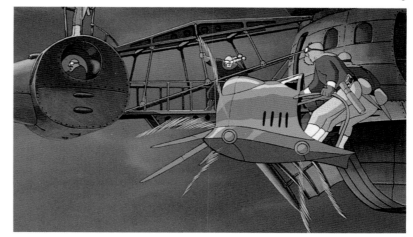

4

5

1

1   *Tiger Moth*. [Initial design]

"The one with arms and legs is something I drew around the beginning,
but the whole world would have changed if I had used this one. It would've
ended up very manga-like.

"In a film, you need ground for the characters to stand on. The ground in
the film world is a boundary to indicate that whatever comes next is not a
lie. Using this initial form would have risked ripping holes in the humanity of
Dola and the others. That's why I toned *Tiger Moth* down to the level you see
in the movie."

2–3   *Tiger Moth*. [Concept sketch]

"Without a gas bag, they can't really relax. They have to always be flying. It's
easy to think up several ways they would come to stop in the sky. I added
the gas bag with the idea of them being able to hover, rather than as part of
some attempt to make a weird vehicle."

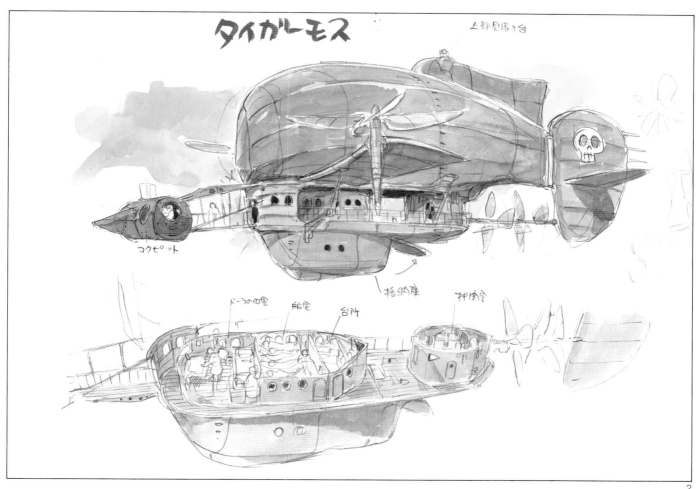

タイガーモス

上部見張り台

コクピット

格納庫

拝官室

ドーラの伯室　船室　台所

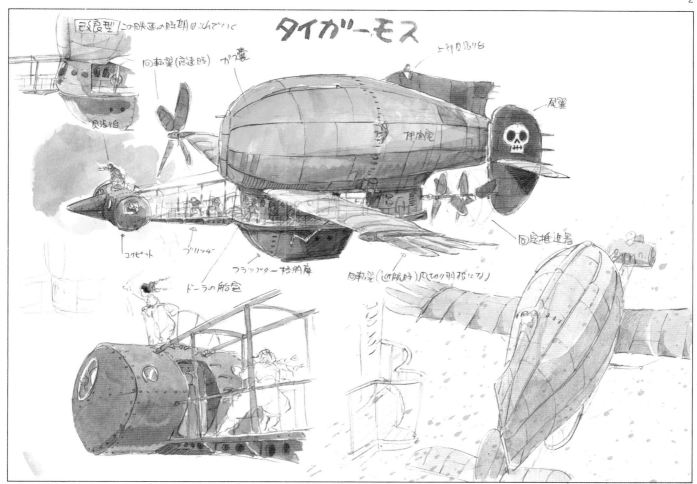

タイガーモス

改良型（この映画の時期はこんでいて

回転翼(高速時)　ガス嚢

上部見張り台

尾翼

見張り台

拝官室

回転推進器

コクピット　プリッジ

フラッター格納庫

ドーラの船室

回転翼(巡航時)ただし羽根になり

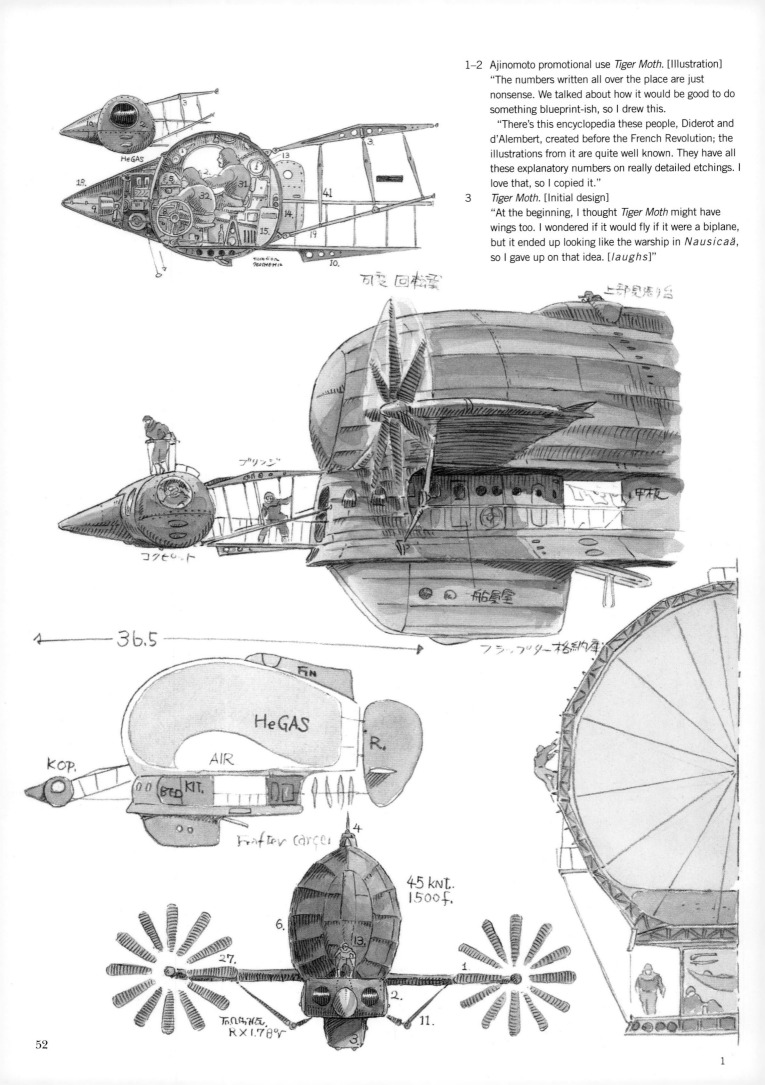

1–2 Ajinomoto promotional use *Tiger Moth*. [Illustration]
"The numbers written all over the place are just nonsense. We talked about how it would be good to do something blueprint-ish, so I drew this.

"There's this encyclopedia these people, Diderot and d'Alembert, created before the French Revolution; the illustrations from it are quite well known. They have all these explanatory numbers on really detailed etchings. I love that, so I copied it."

3 *Tiger Moth*. [Initial design]
"At the beginning, I thought *Tiger Moth* might have wings too. I wondered if it would fly if it were a biplane, but it ended up looking like the warship in *Nausicaä*, so I gave up on that idea. [*laughs*]"

1

27.

watchman

He GAS

KT 19

コナ

2.

エンジンゴム

hesuon
161

ナカラウィハ

4.

15.

6.

27.

27.

13.

11.

2.

2

タイガーモス (2)

3

1

2

1, 4 Pazu's hut. [Concept sketch]
"I wanted to stand Pazu above the chimney. And a regular house
would have been boring, so I made it on top of a hut. But since it
would have been dull to just have the chimney on the roof of the
hut, I drew this with the idea of maybe putting a blast furnace or
something up there.

"With the old factory lot, I thought Pazu would need a large
space since he was putting together that airplane, and so I had the
concept of the hut being built on the remains of the blast furnace."

2   Pazu inside the hut. [Cel]
3   Sheeta sleeping in Pazu's bed. [Film]

3

4

Double mask superimposition

A thin, lingering smoke comes from the chimney of Pazu's hut in the early morning. Instead of drawing the outline of the smoke clearly on the cel, we used a means of making the smoke more hazy. Smoke was drawn onto the cel, and then two masks were laid on top of that. The smoke on the cel continued to move, while the masks were superimposed (double exposed) over Pazu's hut. When cel A with the black coloring in the diagram to the right covers the smoke, the screen is completely black, so nothing is superimposed. Sliding A to the left reveals smoke here and there. By then sliding B at a different speed on top of that, the outline of the smoke drawn on the cel becomes hazy.

The part of superimposition

Brush strokes to make the outline hazy (B)

Cell layer for first starting out (A)

Smoke cel

Background, etc.

1

2

5

3

6

4

1   Pazu's hut. [Initial design]
    "I drew this world in the beginning, a place where airships
    would fly by like this, sort of like ships regularly passing down
    a river."
2–4 Pazu's hut. [Concept sketch]
    "I couldn't really nail down the tower and the hut, so I drew a
    bunch of things."
5   Slag Ravine. [Concept sketch]
6   Pazu's hut. [Film]

1   Pazu's morning routine. [Concept sketch]
"When I said to Kameoka (Osamu) that I
might skip the playing the trumpet part, he
was strongly opposed. 'No, go with that,' he
said. Eventually, Pazu did end up playing
the trumpet. I was pressured into it, you see.
[*laughs*]
    "You think of many different things in the
process of creating a story. At first, I thought
he should play the trumpet, but then I
wondered how it would be if he didn't; you
have this kind of back and forth in yourself
before you come to a decision."
2   Pazu playing the trumpet. [Film]
3, 5–8 Doves flying through the ravine. [Film]
4   Pazu's hut. [Cel]
"In the initial plan, Slag Ravine wasn't
supposed to be as deep a valley as that.
[*laughs*] One of the girls did the layout, and
just as I was thinking maybe it was a little
too deep, Nozaki (Toshiro) had finished it
as an even more incredible space. At first,
I had been thinking of something a little
'gentler,' but then I felt like this was good
the way it was, so this is how it ended up."

3

4

5

7

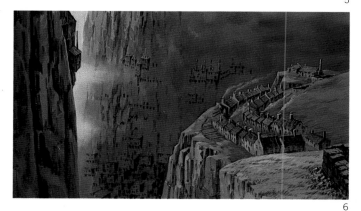

6

8

1

2

1   Pazu looking at sleeping Sheeta. [Novel illustration]
2   Pazu's bedroom. [Concept art]
3   Sheeta getting out of bed. [Film]
       "We argued about the part where she gets out of bed. People
       who had been taught general etiquette said it was weird. They
       said that you wouldn't get up like that if you woke up in a bed
       in someone's house. And when I insisted that it was a perfectly
       natural way of getting up, they suspected I had strange ulterior
       motives. As if with the indecency of a middle-aged man, I had
       perhaps drawn it so you could see her thighs. [*laughs*]"
4–8   Sheeta. [Cel]

3

4

5

6

7

8

1

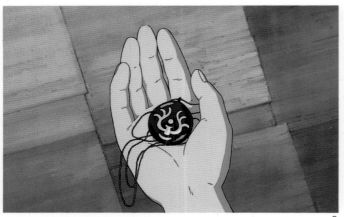

2

3

1   Pazu peering at the etherium crystal. [Novel illustration]
2   Etherium crystal pendant. [Cel]
    "The mark on the etherium crystal is a concept image for a town
    that flies in the sky. A town with wings. The bowl at the bottom
    indicates a semisphere. Drawing the wings in detail would have
    made the animation quite difficult, so we made it more like a
    tree. Trees themselves were not important for the Laputians."
3–8 Pazu testing whether he can fly with the etherium crystal. [Cel]
9   Pazu failing in his experiment and falling into the blast furnace
    remains. [Cel]

4

5

7

6

8

9

オーニソプター
(鳥形飛行機)
実用化されたものは一枚もないが
レオナルド・ダ・ヴィンチ以来ずーっと
夢みられて来た。

1

1   Ornithopter. [Concept sketch]

"Given this form, I think it might just fly even now. It probably only needs something like the auxiliary wings of the archaeopteryx. You don't get the impression at all that it's flying in drawings unless the one wing is lowered when the other is raised. It's fine when it's gliding, but it's a problem when the wings are flapping. It's just not convincing unless there's three or so sets of wings.

"Normally, when you want to fly like a bird in a movie, it's different from flapping the wings and flying like a sparrow. It's more like a black kite tracing out a smooth arc. So that ends up coming out even with fixed wings."

2   Ornithopter being put together. [Concept sketch]

"I first thought about having him go to Sheeta in Gondoa in the last scene. But there was the problem of how to make it fly I mentioned earlier, and after I considered things like whether or not Pazu would succeed on his first try when most inventors have any number of failures, I decided not to make it fly in the end."

2

3–5 Ornithopter being put together. [Film]
6   Pazu making a model fly. [Cel]
7   Pazu talking about his dream with Sheeta. [Cel]
"I wasn't originally against the idea of taking it out and flying. It's just that bringing it out would make the 'ground' of the story into something lighter. And what I mean by that is, if a boy were able to make something like this, then an adult would be able to make it even more easily."

3

4

5

6

1

2

4

3

187

6

7

8

1–2 Laputa shot by Pazu's father. [Cel]
3 Sheeta looking at the photos on the wall. [Cel]
4 Pazu's father taking a picture of Laputa. [Film]
5 Notebook with record of Laputa. [Cel]
6 Notebook. [Film]
7 Sheeta listening to Pazu. [Film]
8 Pazu telling Sheeta about Laputa. [Cel]

1   Pazu and Sheeta running from their
    pursuers. [Cel]
2   Sheeta as her hat goes flying. [Cel]
3   Dola's three sons. [Cel]
4   Boss and Pazu facing the pirates. [Cel]

4

金夫達　　　　　親方　　　　おかみさん

チビのマッジ

5

6

7

帰えんな
ここには貪三人しか
いねえ

やみが‼

9

8

5　People of the mine town. [Concept sketch]
6　Pazu getting ready to face the pirates. [Cel]
7　Boss's wife. [Film]
　　"The wife is twenty years old. Even now, people at the working-class level will
　　get married at fifteen-ish, so I figured about twenty would be good."
8　Pazu being told to protect Sheeta by the wife. [Film]
9　Charles vs. Boss. [Concept sketch]

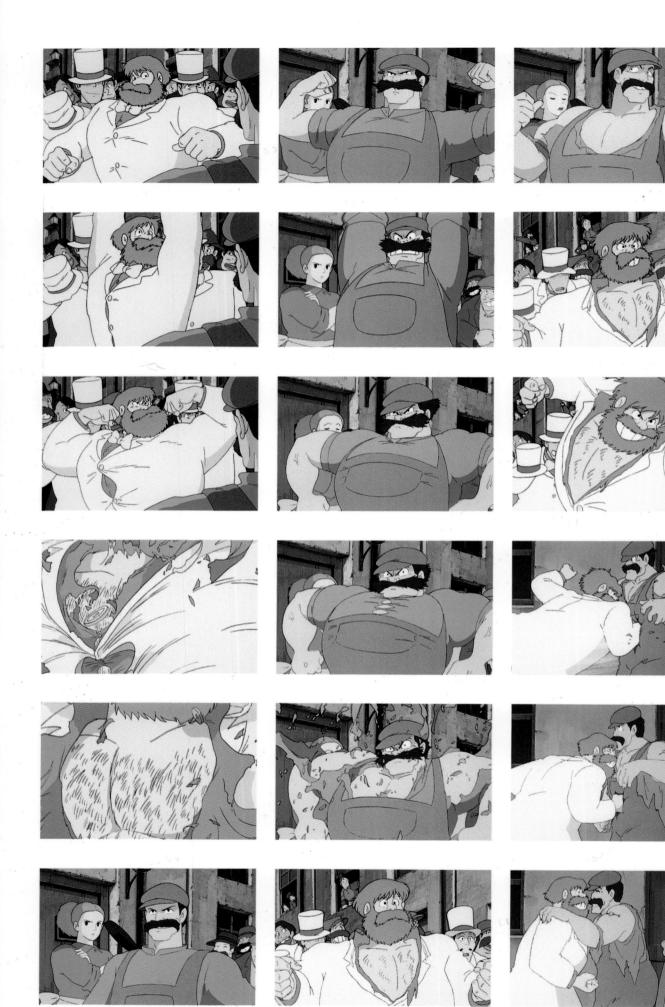

1 Fight between Charles and Boss. [Film]
2 Brawl. [Cel]

"Right from the start, I intended to make the fight scene very manga-like. [laughs]

"I kept pushing the lead (Yoshinori Kaneda) to gradually make it more reckless. [laughs] I knew from the beginning that this would not be one of the scenes with a sense of reality."

1

2

1

2

3

4

5

7

6

1–3 Slag Ravine. [Concept sketch]
"From a fairly early stage, I intended to have a train running along.
If I hadn't had this design in the beginning, I don't think there
would have been the chase on the bridge."

4 Various machines. [Initial design]

5 Military pursuing Sheeta. [Concept sketch]
"I thought of a story where they run away, chased by the military.
I was thinking I'd put Sheeta in disguise and have them get on a
regular passenger train, and then the military aircraft would come
zooming in and Pazu would be dumbfounded.
   "But I figured that having the military appear like that at the
beginning would make the story too big, so I gave up on that.
The military charging in at the beginning looking for the etherium
crystal actually feels real, but I tried it with just the pirates. The
military appearing first would have made the lead too long. And I
also felt like I could draw all kinds of details, like Pazu losing his
job for sheltering Sheeta, so I abandoned that pretty quickly."

6 The pair planning their escape using the light railway. [Concept
sketch]

7 The pair climbing onto the train. [Film]

73

1

2

1–2 Slag Ravine. [Concept art]
3–6 Slag Ravine. [Background]

4

3

5

6

1

1–3 Dola. [Cel]
4–5 Dola. [Initial design]

"Up to now, quite a number of fathers have appeared in my work, but this is the first mother. But when I say 'mother,' rather than the warm, kind mom figure, she's the sort of mother who'll give a bad kid a kick and do what she can to help if she sees something in you. I wanted to use the sort of adult who's critical and loud, but will also think 'kid, get in there' when she sees her child burning with passion. Otherwise, the story would end up being the type of thing where the villain quickly falls in love with the heroine and offers her a flower made of tissue. [*laughs*] Although no matter how many times I use that one, I still like it. [*laughs*]

"If I had put a man in the role of the pirate captain, I think it would've ended up like that. The story would've turned into them kidnapping Sheeta and then trying to woo her or something. [*laughs*] That itself would be interesting, but at any rate, that's why I decided to make it a mother this time.

"This story is about a boy and a girl setting out on an adventure and meeting different adults along the way. So I wanted to have a very adult adult, and I came up with Dola. Unparalleled appetite, magnificent greed, robust health."

2

3

1

2

5

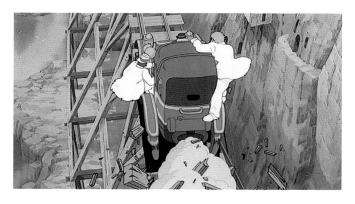

4

1–4 Dola's automobile chasing Sheeta. [Film]
5   Automobile. [Cel]
     "Dola's got more energy than her sons, who are younger than
     she is. And I thought a bunch of different things about this
     too. Things like what it would be like if she was carried on
     her kids' backs. It's just that ever since *The Twilight Years*,
     the issue of the elderly has been taken quite seriously. So I
     thought it wouldn't be such a bad idea to have a senior citizen
     who was tougher than the young people around her. [*laughs*]"

3

1

2

3

4

5

7

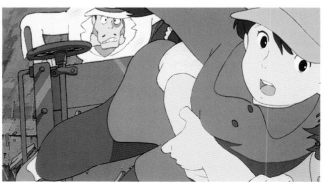

1   Pazu and Sheeta fleeing. [Concept sketch]
2   Armored train on the elevated rail line. [Film]
3   Pazu and Sheeta staring at the armored train. [Film]
4–5 Armored train. [Cel]
6   Pazu and Sheeta running from the pirates. [Film]
7   The pair hanging from the elevated rail line. [Cel]

1

2

1 Etherium crystal activation. [Film]
2 The pair descending to the tunnel. [Cel]

1–2 Slag Ravine. [Background]
3   The pair descending to the tunnel. [Film]
4   Slag Ravine. [Concept art]

4

1   Sheeta and Pazu descending to the tunnel. [Cel]
2–6   Pazu lighting a lamp. [Film]
7   The pair walking in the tunnel. [Cel]
8–10   Inside the tunnel. [Concept sketch]
       "I considered having a place where the etherium crystal
       was flashing in a place where they were lost, but I
       eventually abandoned that."

8

9

10

1–3 Pazu and Sheeta having a meal.
  [Film]
4 Yaku and Sheeta. [Concept sketch]
  "I drew this instead of a character
  design for the character of Yaku."
5 Yaku and Sheeta. [Cel]
6 Gondoan valley. [Background]

1

2

4

3

1–2 Uncle Pom. [Concept sketch]

"For this character, I added Yoshifumi Kondo and Yasuji Mori together and then divided by two. [*laughs*]
The personality of this character Pom is that he's shy in front of people and can't talk. He's someone who would rather spend time with the rocks underground than talk with people.

"Even when he sees the etherium crystal, he says it's 'too strong.' His hands tremble and shake, and he understands of course the terrifying power hidden in the stone. That's why he can say that to Sheeta. [Pom's dialogue is noted on P93.]

"He's not world-wise. I designed him with the idea that for however bad he is at making a living in the world, he's a person who realizes what's most important."

3 Pazu discovering Uncle Pom. [Film]
4 Uncle Pom. [Cel]
5 Inside the tunnel. [Background]
6–7 The pair talking with Uncle Pom. [Film]
8 Uncle Pom talking about the etherium crystal. [Cel]

1

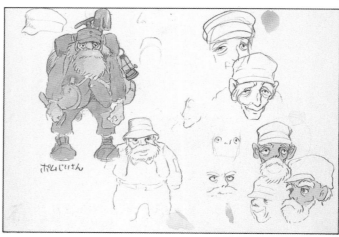

2

3

5

6

7

8

Glass dust superimposition

Etherium glitters like galaxies on the surface of the rock wall of the underground abandoned mine. To express this ephemeral beauty, our first thought was glass dust superimposition. We tried to have the dust of finely crushed glass catch the light and superimpose an irregular reflection, but the data was just too irregular and we were forced to give up on that.

So we made a lith film with holes jabbed in it like stars at night and did a double exposure with transmitted light.

In the end, we didn't use the glass dust, but the name at least hung around right until the end.

Mixed color overlap

The magic of the etherium, light seeping out from the rock cross-section. To express this light—bright in the center and gradually becoming darker toward the edges—mixed-color overlap was proposed.

In the movie, the scene is drawn so that the ring of light spreads out as it moves from the inside to the outside. But with this, the bright surface is small in the beginning and then pushed to the outside, meaning it simply spreads out the way it is, without the color changing. So we made the same picture shades darker and overlaid these images. And when we did, magic! As the ring of light moved outward, the color mixed with the overlay to gradually become darker, giving a sense of the etherium stone becoming a regular rock when it touches the air.

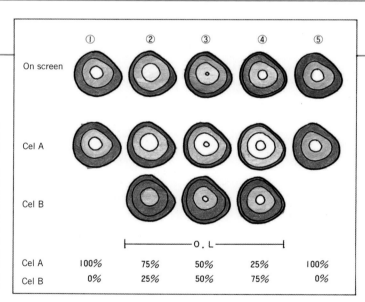

	①	②	③	④	⑤
On screen					
Cel A					
Cel B					
Cel A	100%	75%	50%	25%	100%
Cel B	0%	25%	50%	75%	0%

O. L

1

2

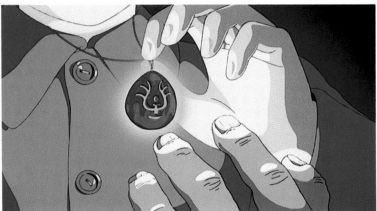

3

1–3 Uncle Pom talking about etherium. [Film]
Pom: "That crystal is extremely powerful, but with a power that rightfully belongs to the earth from which it came. To forget that and then try and use the crystal's power for selfish reasons will bring great unhappiness. You understand? Your crystal should remind us that we come from the earth..."

1

2

3

1–2 Parting from Uncle Pom. [Film]
3   Sheeta telling Pazu her real name. [Cel]
4   Pazu delighted to learn that Laputa really
     exists. [Cel]
5–7 Military rocket chasing Sheeta. [Film]
8   Rocket closing in on the pair. [Novel
     illustration]

4

5

6

7

8

1

4

2

1–3　Rocket. [Concept sketch]

"I had planned to have the rocket fly off from the bottom of *Goliath* (see *Goliath* P115), but I gave up on that because of the needs of the storyboard.

"And at first, they were going to fly in a pulsed rocket, but the role of the rocket turned out differently, so it ended up just flying like a bird. It's also larger than I had initially anticipated. Because at any rate, Muska is coming out of it. I actually had the concept of a fighter plane, but it gradually turned into a passenger plane.

"I thought that when it flew, it would take off chugging when you lit the fire with a match. I'm really attracted to engines like that. The way you have to take off the stopcock when starting and light the fire with a match.

But there was nowhere to put that. Someday, somewhere, I would like to use it…"

4　Rockets turning on top of the hill. [Film]

3

5 Tedus fort. [Film]
6 Tedus fort. [Concept sketch]
7 Old Tedus fortress and Tochkas. [Film]
8 Tedus fort. [Concept sketch]

"The eight bumps around the fort are anti-tank obstacles. This is a time when there were no tanks or anything, but I wanted to use them for distance from the town. The fort's a result of going to Wales, something along the lines of an old castle. Although the truth is this sort of fort is flat. [*laughs*]"

5

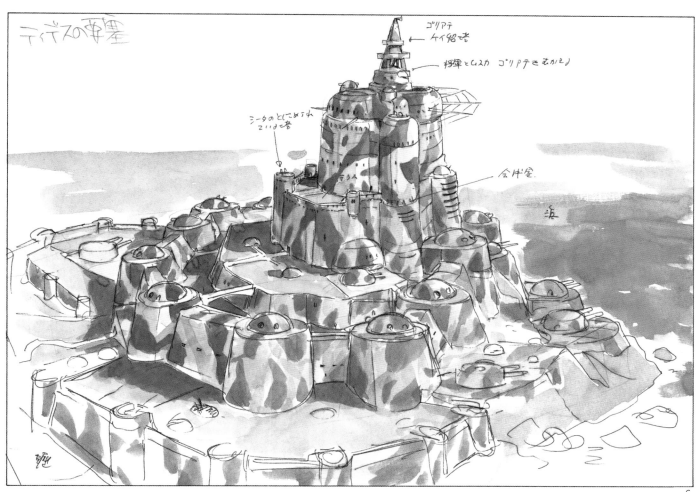

6

7

8

1

2

3

1, 4   Muska. [Cel]
2   Military soldier. [Concept sketch]
3   Muska. [Initial design]
       "In the beginning, I decided to make Muska's face square, and
       he ended up looking exactly like Lepka. We said he was Lepka's
       ancestor, things like that. [*laughs*]

       "Eventually, with the idea of making him younger than Lepka,
       I settled on a longer, thinner, sort of vegetal face. Lepka and
       Cagliostro are, in a sense, complete men. In contrast, it seemed
       to me that Muska is not quite finished. I designed him as a man
       who joined the military because he has ambition, but who also
       has a serious complex about something. Originally, he boasted
       of being from a noble family, but there's a gap between this and
       how he's actually nothing more than a tiny part of the military.

       "So there were several things like this, and he also had the
       inner ambition to 'find it someday.' So he had to be a younger
       person. But he couldn't be a stupid greenhorn, and he ended up
       having this sort of organic intellectual feel."
5   Sheeta and Muska. [Film]
6   Sheeta locked up in a room in Tedus. [Cel]
7   Room Sheeta is locked up in. [Background]

4

5

6

7

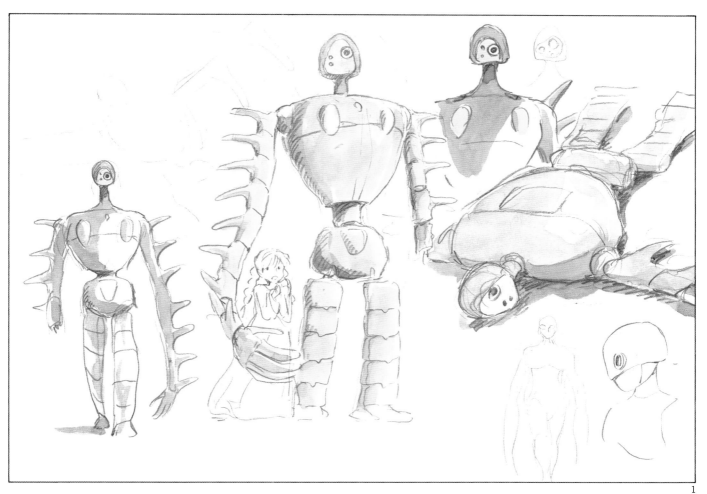

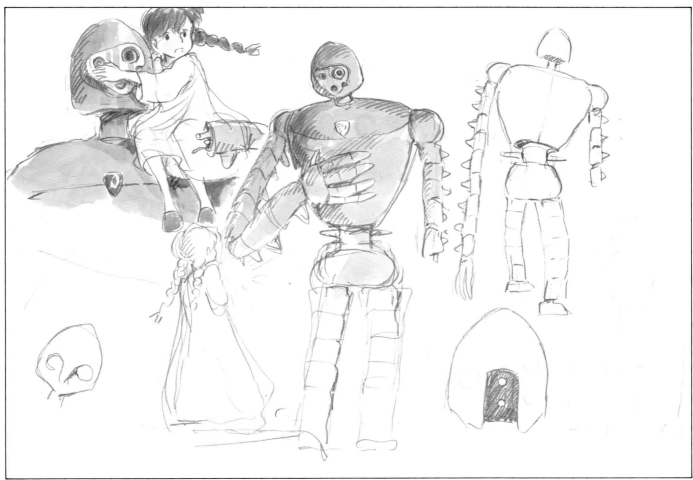

3

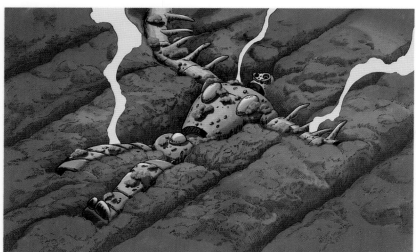

4

1–2 Robot soldier. [Concept sketch]
"When you take the back off of a clock, it's a strange feeling; there's a whole machine tucked in there. The design of the face comes from that. I like it and actually used it once for TV (last episode of *Lupin III Part II*), but it's lingered in my head for some reason, and so I tried using it again here. I had decided right from the beginning of planning to have this robot in the movie. Because I was thinking about not just showing the robot soldiers, but also another aspect of the Laputian culture, a brutal part."

3–5 Fallen robot soldier. [Cel]
"You're going to ask me why the robot fell, aren't you? Then I'll say that it got caught in a crumbling building and came falling down like that. [laughs] In that case, there should have been stones falling too, but I guess those fell into the sea. Although there's also the theory that the building collapsed and came falling down when it was hit by a meteor. [*laughs*]"

6 Robot soldier's broken arm. [Film]

6

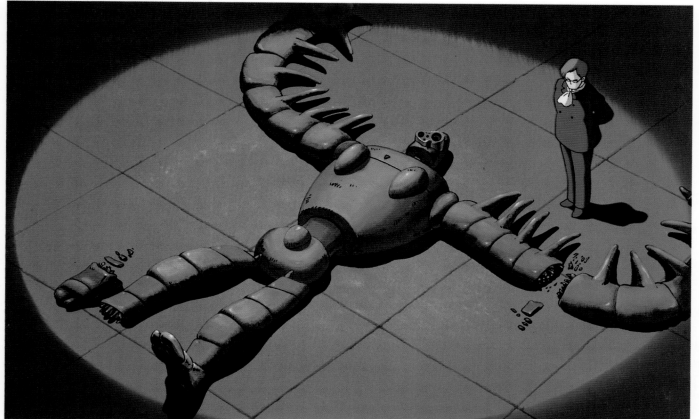

5

1

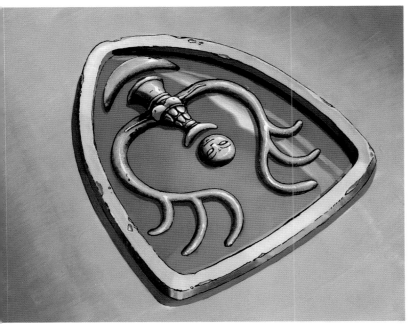

2

3

4

5

1   Muska displaying the etherium crystal. [Cel]
2   Laputian crest. [Cel]
3–8 Sheeta and Muska. [Film]
9   Muska. [Cel]

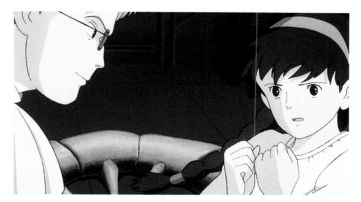

7

6

8   9

1   Sheeta. [Cel]
2–5 Sheeta telling Pazu goodbye. [Film]
6   Tedus fort. [Background]
7   Boss's daughter Madge. [Film and cel]
8   Mine residence tenement houses. [Film]

6

8

7

1

2

3

4

1   Pazu tied up by the pirates. [Novel illustration]
2   Pazu. [Cel]
3–5 Dola. [Film]
6   Flaptor takeoff. [Film]

5

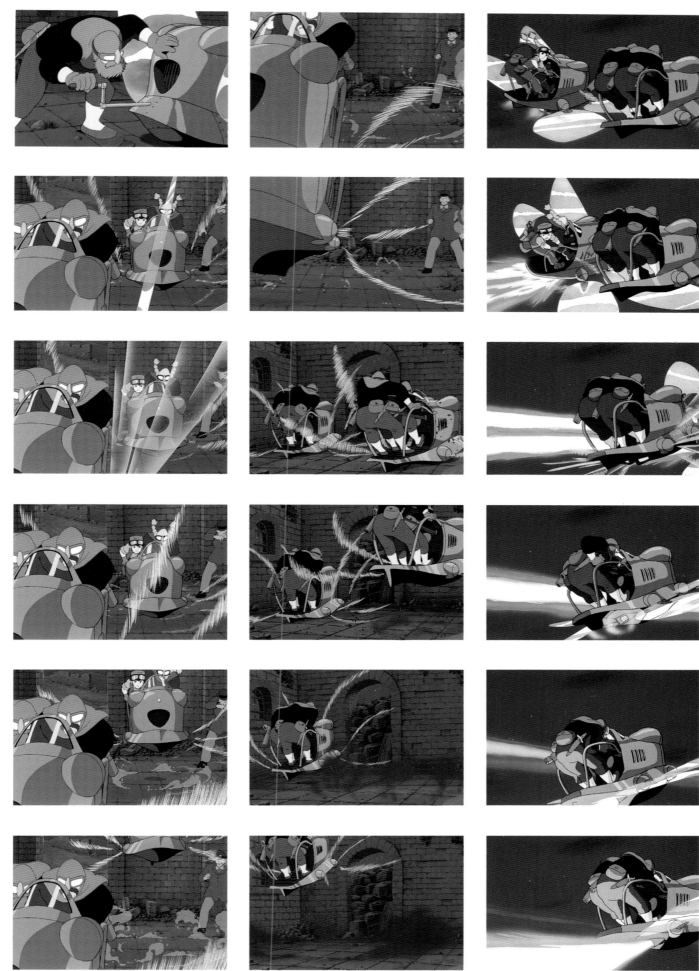

フラップター

1   Flaptor. [Design]
2–4 Flaptor. [Concept sketch]
5   Flaptor. [Yoshinori Kaneda initial design]

"Ornithopter is an actual word, but no matter which way you look at it, the flaptor is shaped like an insect, so I couldn't very well call it an ornithopter. So I was left wondering what to do. It flies by flapping furiously, so I combined ornithopter with the word 'flap' and came up with flaptor.

"I had Kaneda work out the movement pattern. It has claws in the design, and at first, we were thinking of having it grab on with the claws when coming into contact with the airship. (See 3.) But that would have taken too much work, so we gave up on it. You don't want to add any extra bits when animating, so we took off the claws.

"The impact would have been too great if the flaptor wings were made to move in a circular motion with a crank, so I thought maybe the scientist (Dola's husband) went and got a bunch of muscles from frogs or something and stimulated them with electricity to make the wings flap.

"It just didn't look like they were flying, however, and eventually we did them how they are in the film. I really wanted to make the wings flap to fly, but that was indeed too difficult."

2

3

4

5

Flaptor Test

Flaptor: Machine that flies around freely, moving forward, ascending, suddenly descending, and stopping in midair with the flapping of its four wings. The idea was not a leisurely flapping of large wings like with the Ohm that appear in *Nausicaä of the Valley of the Wind*, but rather something more angular. Director Miyazaki noted, "They buzz through the air like a fly, suddenly stop, and change directions like that."

The first job Miyazaki assigned to lead animator Yoshinori Kaneda, who joined Ghibli in August, was the flaptor test.

The flaptor test was roughly divided into two—the wing flapping test (part 1) and the dry brush (touch) test (part 2)—and twelve to sixteen different patterns were thought up for each of these. We'll take a look here at some representative examples in order.

Flapping 1 frame, 8 images repeated (Fig. 1)

The fastest flapping is with four images. The flapping of the wings is repeated up, center, down, center, and then up again. However, if this was shot with one frame, rather than looking like flapping, it would end up looking like the four wings were appearing and disappearing in the same place. This happens because in one second, you see the same pictures six or seven times, and your eyes can't capture that the wings are moving. Thus, the repetition was made with eight images: up, center, down, center, up, center, down, center, and finally up. Naturally, they were all different images. This made it so that the same picture was seen only three times a second, which is when it's thought the eye loses track of the image. However, even with the wings flapping six times a second like those of a fly, it wouldn't work if the wings were flapping at a speed the eye couldn't catch when we actually shot and looked at the film. It was too slow.

Fig. 1. 1 frame, 8 images, repeated.

1 frame, 8 images, randomly!

It felt slow because you could follow the movement of the wings with your eyes. So here, we used the previous eight wing images, mixed up the order (randomly), and shot that, but this didn't work either. It just turned out impossible to understand what was what.

1 frame, four images, blurring (Fig. 2)

In animation, there's a technique called blurring. After something moving quickly, you draw a light afterimage and add in the speed that's too fast for the eye to follow. However, unless we changed the number of times the wings flapped in a second, this was also not going to work. We did try mixing into the blur pattern smaller and larger wings (Fig. 3), but this ended up looking like the flaptor was firing a machine gun or something, and of course, this made Kaneda and everyone else groan.

Thus, the flaptor's wings went from flapping in the images to touches with a dry brush. The brushing itself wasn't a problem. Smudging on two repeating images was enough to give the impression that here the wings were flapping busily. Which is to say, we succeeded in making the flaptor fly like a buzzing insect.

We succeeded in making it fly, but for the audience, who would have no idea how a flaptor flew, just these touches wouldn't be sufficient to explain it.

We obsessed over many different tricks to try and

Fig. 2. 1 frame, 4 images, repeated/blurring.

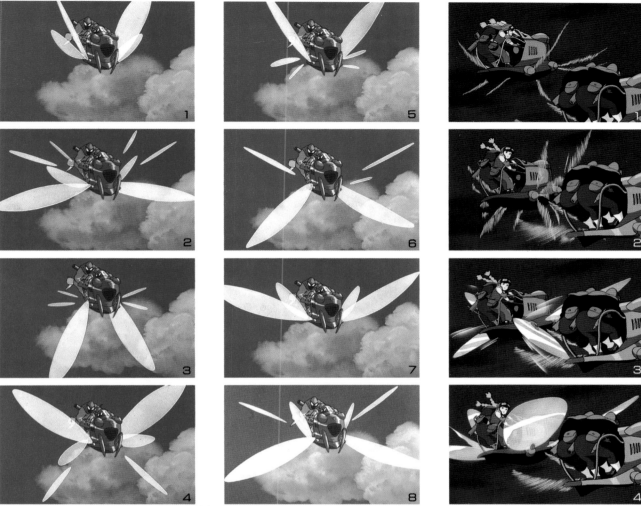

Fig. 3. 1 frame, 8 images, repeated.　　　　　　　　　Fig. 4. Wings stopping abruptly.

show that it was flying by flapping its wings, such as stopping the wings while the flaptor was buzzing along and having it glide (Fig. 4), or accelerating with a booster while the wings were stopped and then having them start flapping again.

It wasn't just the animation side obsessing over this. Color designer Michiyo Yasuda hurried to set the colors for the flaptor, even though the characters still weren't set. She tested out whether to paint the flaptor wings or brush them or to double expose them, and she also noted that she couldn't set just one color for the dry brushing. She discovered that the colors would have to change from scene to scene, or even within a single shot, depending on the light source. Meanwhile, Miyazaki, who was in the middle of creating the storyboard, changed the flapping in the storyboard to the dry brushing, so you could say it was an essential test for all parts.

Also, when all the shots were animated, with the flaptors coming toward the foreground or moving into the background, it was initially thought that the flaptor body would have one set of in-betweens and the wings alone would have special flaptor wing in-betweening. The idea was that the flapping needed its own special images for the inbetweens. Because we eventually settled on the dry brushing, a stop was put to this particular test.

And this is how flaptors came to buzz through the air.

◄ An actual example of how the groping in the dark with the flaptors was not only used in animation and finishing. At the point when it was decided that the wings would be handled with dry brushing, the storyboard had already advanced quite far, to Pazu heading toward Tedus fort to rescue Sheeta. Thus, the flaptor wings clearly written into the attack scene at the beginning of the movie in the storyboard as well were handled with the drybrushing around the time when Pazu sets out (?!) on Dola's flaptor.

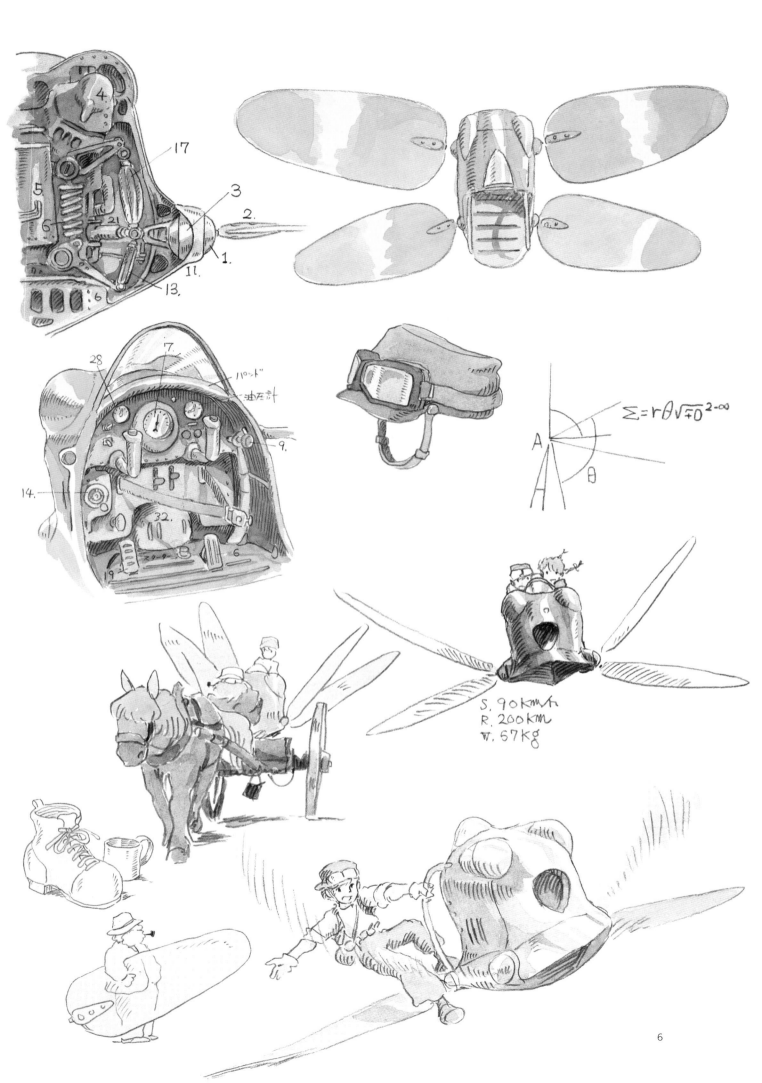

$$\Sigma = r\theta\sqrt{\mp 0}^{2-\infty}$$

S. 90km/h
R. 200km
W. 67kg

4

5

1, 5   *Goliath*. [Cel]
2–4   *Goliath*. [Film]
6   *Goliath*. [Concept sketch]
       "There were other proposals for the
       design of *Goliath*. I kept them from
       the staff, just drawing in secret the
       shapes that I wanted it to have. And
       then it ended up being something
       completely not out of place, even
       though I could have had any old weird
       thing flying around in the world of
       the movie. I accidentally gave it a
       respectable sort of shape. It's a simple
       thing, as long as you get your ideas in
       groups. [*laughs*]"

114

1

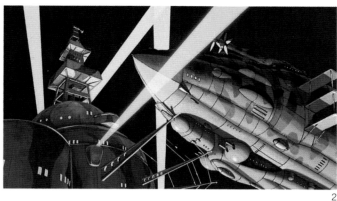

2

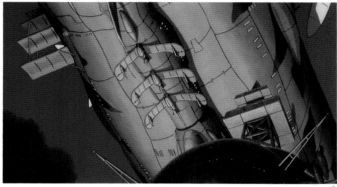

3

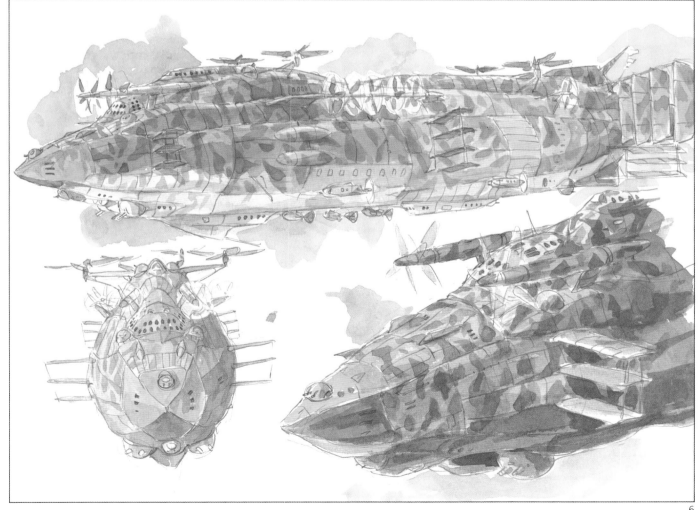

1–3 Sheeta in her youth being taught the spell by her grandmother. [Cel]

4 Sheeta chanting the spell, "Leetay Latuparita Ulus Aria Los Balu Netoreel" [Cel]

5–6 Etherium crystal emitting light. [Film]

1

2

3

4

5

6

1

3

1   Muska stunned at the activation of the
    etherium crystal. [Cel]
2   Muska getting something like a shock when
    touching the etherium crystal. [Film]
3   Sheeta stepping back in fear. [Film]
4–5 Robot soldier beginning to move. [Cel]
6   Robot soldier moving. [Film]
7   Sheeta afraid. [Film]

2

4

5

7

6

1

1   Robot soldier standing in the middle of the flames. [Cel]
2   Robot soldier flying. [Film]
    "The wings come out and are pulled back in, so anything
    hard is out of the question. So we say the robot soldier's body
    is some kind of metal rubber. [*laughs*]"

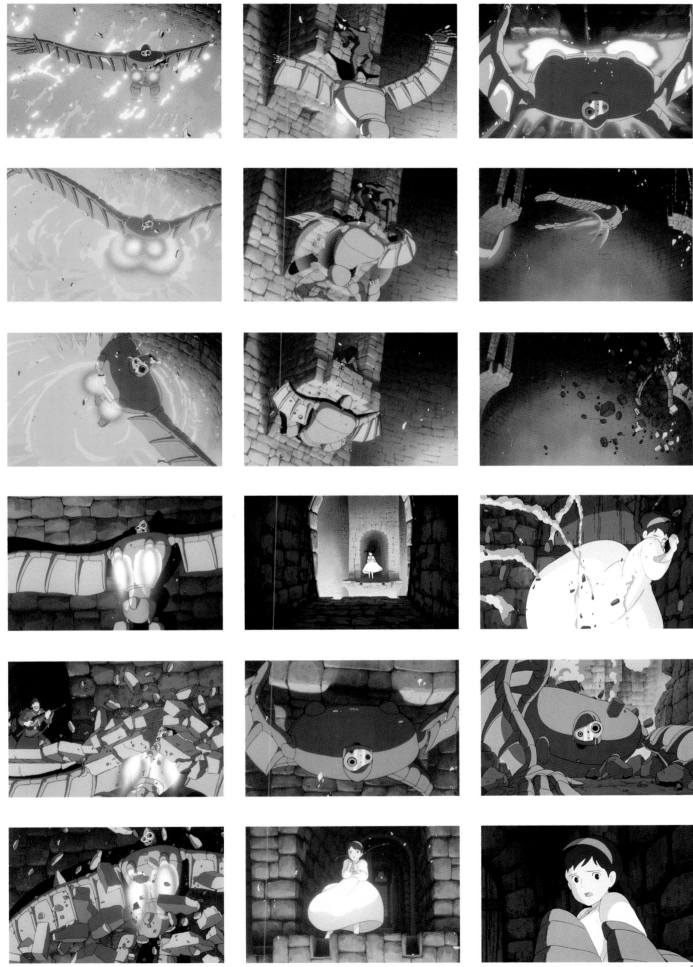

1

2

4

5

1   Light of the etherium crystal showing the
    location of Laputa. [Film]
2   Robot soldier and Sheeta. [Film]
3   Robot soldier protecting Sheeta like a fierce
    god. [Cel]
4   Muska directing strategy on the phone.
    [Cel]
5   Sheeta. [Film]

3

1

2

3

4

1 Pazu on his way to get Sheeta back. [Cel]
2 Pazu reaching his hand out and Sheeta trying to take it. [Film]
3 Pazu shouting "Sheeta, my hand. Take it!" [Cel]
4 Sheeta lifting her face at Pazu's voice. [Cel]
5 Robot soldier destroyed by *Goliath* after standing Sheeta on the parapet. [Film]
6 The robot soldier stretching a hand out to Sheeta as its body is enveloped in flames. [Film]
7 Sheeta, unable to do anything but hold its finger. [Cel]

5

6   7

1 Pazu facing his last chance to rescue Sheeta. [Cel]

2 Flaptor charging into Tedus now. [Film]

3 Sheeta standing in the middle of strong winds and flames, calling out "Pazu." [Film]

4 Pazu grabbing tightly on to Sheeta. [Film]

5–6 Muska getting the etherium crystal and reflecting on it gleefully. [Film]

7 Robot soldier, completely burned. [Film]

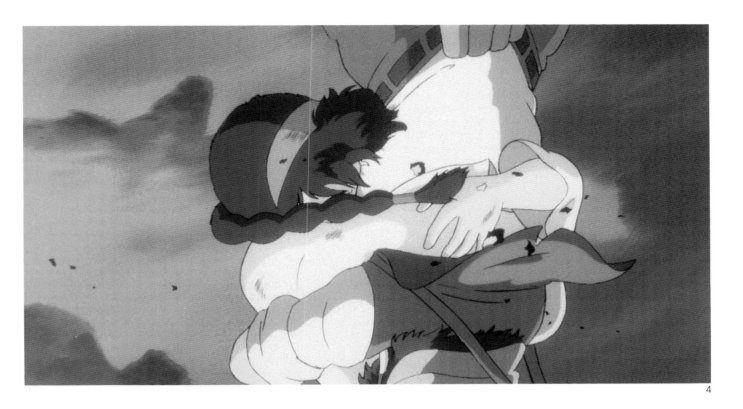

4

5

6

7

1

2

1   Pazu after rescuing Sheeta. [Concept sketch]
2   The pair deciding to go to Laputa. [Cel]
3–4 The pair looking at the doves and Pazu's hut. [Cel]
5   Pazu's hut. [Background]

3

4

5

1

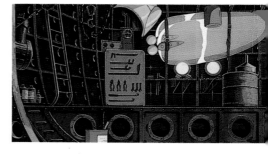

3

1   *Tiger Moth* lifting off from between rocky
     mountains the ocean can be seen from. [Cel]
2   *Tiger Moth* flying through the clouds. [Film]
3   Flaptor being taken into *Tiger Moth*. [Film]

2

1

2

3

1　Motoro. [Cel]

"At first, this character didn't have a name. I just called him 'old man,' but then Kameoka (Osamu) asked me was his name was. I replied 'old man,' and he said, 'That's not helpful,' so that's when I gave it some thought. There's this old Toei Animation film *Mogura no Motoro*; I took the name from that.

"At any rate, since this is a character I hadn't initially planned on having, I didn't do anything in the way of design. When we were animating, I just said, 'Look at the storyboard and draw that.' [*laughs*] The reason I put this character in was because I wanted to have a training period for Pazu. Right from the start, Pazu's function on this voyage was to become a boy who understands what he has to do. I thought of it as being the same as going out into the real world. So there had to be a character who knew that the boy was doing things properly, which is where Motoro comes in. I was right to put him in. And his voice is also great."

2　Motoro playing chess with Dola. [Cel]

"Someone on the staff said to me, 'I'm so glad Dola's not all alone.' This is a result of introducing Motoro; there was no one on *Tiger Moth* in the same age group as Dola. And with even just one person her own age, Dola stops being a lonely person."

3 Pazu helping Motoro in the engine room. [Film]
4 Sheeta being given a change of clothes in Dola's room. [Cel]
5 Dola using the abacus. [Cel]
6 Dola. [Character notes]

1

2

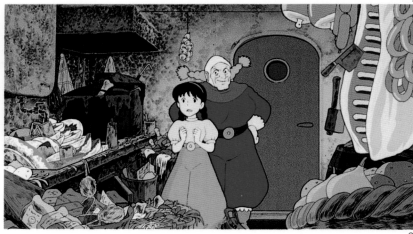

3

1, 6–7 Sheeta in the mess. [Cel]
2   Sheeta almost blown away by a fierce wind.
        [Film]
3   Sheeta stunned at how dirty the mess is.
        [Film]
4   Sheeta holding up Dola's clothing in
        surprise. [Cel]
5   Sheeta cutting ingredients up into a large
        pot. [Film]

4

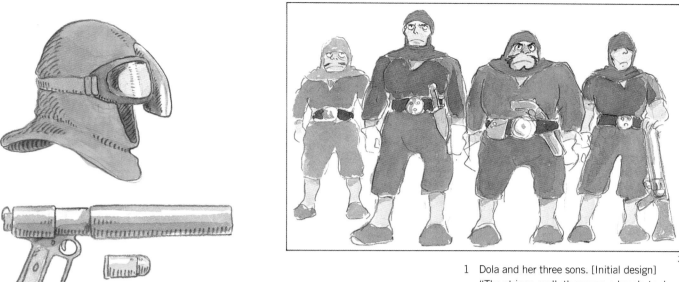

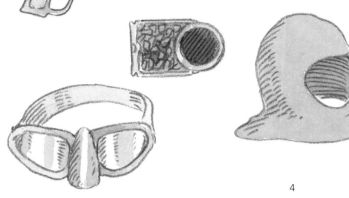

3

4

1   Dola and her three sons. [Initial design]
    "The stripes, well, they were a hassle to draw.
    Even if we did go ahead and keep them, we
    expected that the stripes would move and ruin
    things, so I ended up taking them out."

2   Sons and subordinate characters. [Notes]
    "I took the names for Dola's three sons from
    kings of France. "However much Charles
    might have that kind of idiot aspect to him, I
    wanted him to also be seen as having a serious
    face sometimes. There was this security guard
    at one building we went to in Wales who had
    a really good face. This large man, two meters
    tall, was patrolling with a German shepherd.
    At first glance, his face was scary, but he
    actually had a simple, good face. At that time,
    I thought, ooh, that's the sort of face I want.

    "Louis, well, he's the product of Dola having
    an affair with a good man in Spain, and when
    you put those faces together, that's what you
    get. [laughs] Et cetera. I thought of all kinds of
    silly things when I was drawing him.

    "The one I had the most trouble with was
    Henry. And this is the reason why there's
    nothing particularly noteworthy about his face.
    When we were doing the actual work on the
    movie, I'd forget what he looked like. [laughs]

    "The subordinates are Ka, Ki, Ku, Ke, and
    Ko. I like Ko. When the coloring was done, he
    actually ended up having a weird face, so right
    away, I went to talk with the staff about putting
    him onscreen. And in the end, Ko was the only
    one we managed to use."

3   Three sons and subordinates. [Initial design]
    "This picture is from around the beginning, so
    Charles is really quite different."

4   Pirate equipment. [Ajinomoto advertisement
    illustration]

5   Curious about Sheeta, the sons and
    subordinates were standing and listening at
    the mess door, but…[Cel]

6   One of the five daily meals. [Cel]
    "About the relationship between the sons and
    the subordinates, Dola doesn't discriminate
    between her sons and her crew. She makes
    her sons do hard jobs too. Maybe in truth, one
    of those subordinates is also her son. [laughs]
    Some people have asked if all of the crew
    members are her sons, you know."

5

6

1 *Tiger Moth* heading for the full moon. [Cel]
2 Strangely bright for Sheeta climbing up to the lookout. [Cel]
3 Sheeta waking up at the sound of Pazu and Louis talking. [Film]
4 Sheeta leaving Dola's room to go out onto the deck. [Film]
5 Pazu moving to put the blanket he's wearing around Sheeta, who's shivering with the chill of the night wind. [Film]
6 Sheeta confessing her anxiety about going to Laputa. [Cel]
   Sheeta: "I wish I'd thrown the crystal away."
   Pazu: "But then we never would have met."
7 Sheeta taking heart at Pazu's words and smiling. [Film]
8 Pazu encouraging Sheeta with a face like the sun in the moonlit night. [Film]
9 Dola listening to the pair talking through the speaking tube. [Cel]
   (There is no privacy on this ship. [From the storyboard])

6

7

8

9

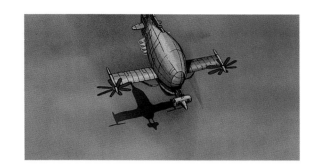

1

2

3

1   *Goliath* appearing directly below *Tiger Moth*. [Film]
2   *Tiger Moth* dodging to the right on an incline. [Cel]
3   *Goliath* coming up like a giant whale. [Cel]
4   Opening fire on *Tiger Moth* while illuminating the ship with a searchlight. [Film]
5   Etherium crystal emitting a pale blue light on top of the compass. [Film]
6–7   Muska and the officers on the bridge of *Goliath*. [Cel]

4

5

6

7

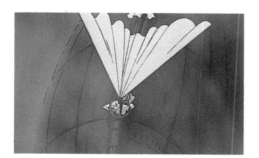

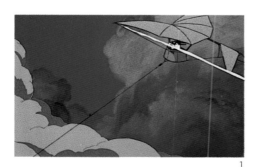

2

3

1

4

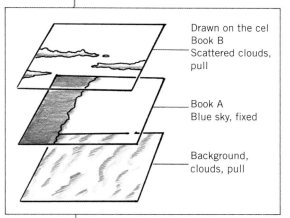

Drawn on the cel
Book B
Scattered clouds,
pull

Book A
Blue sky, fixed

Background,
clouds, pull

6

Hurricane

Method devised to express the swirling tower of clouds:

There was nothing. Just clouds being pulled out from under the blue sky placed on top.

Things in the distance hide in the shadows of things that are closer (naturally). To express this in animation, you solve the problem by layering the cells, with things in the distance on the bottom and things closer on top. In accordance with this theory, since the clouds should be more up front than the blue sky, they would have to go on top. And here is the reversal of the idea. If we pull the clouds from under the blue sky, wouldn't it look as though it were rotating? And that is where the technique was born.

1   The pair ascending up into the sky using the lookout as a kite. [Film]
2   Sheeta clinging to Pazu, battered by the fierce wind. [Film]
3   Pazu and Sheeta dance though the sky as a kite to discover *Goliath*. [Cel]
4   They should have been flying to the east, but the sun is rising from the side. [Cel]
5   Hurricane. [Background]
6   The pair surprised, seeing the hurricane. [Film]

1 *Tiger Moth* damaged in *Goliath*'s
   attack. [Film]
   "In this scene, Motoro comes
   running out from the engine room.
   Did you notice that? Just as I
   was coming up on this scene, I
   thought, aah, Motoro's dead, and
   then I quickly decided to have him
   escape."
2 *Goliath* approaching from *Tiger
   Moth*'s rear. [Film]
3 *Tiger Moth* under attack from
   Goliath. [Film]
4 A twisted smile comes across
   Muska's face. [Cel]
   Muska: "The light is pointing to the
   center of the whirlwind. Laputa is in
   that storm."

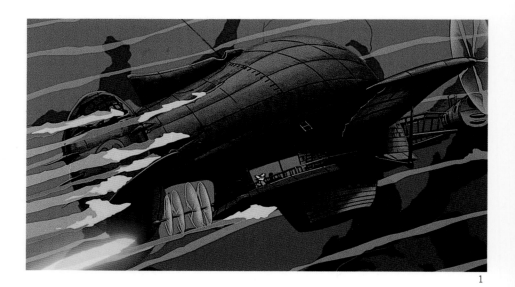

1

2

3

4

5

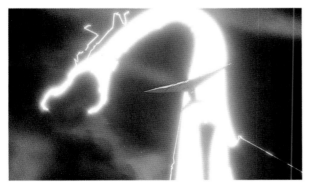

7

5   Entering the Hurricane, Pazu sees a vision of his father. [Cel]

6   Vision of Pazu's father, appearing as if to guide Pazu. The kite Pazu and Sheeta are riding on passes through a corridor of lightning. [Film]

7   *Tiger Moth* flying through a calm. [Concept sketch]

6

1

4

1–3 Laputa. [Concept sketch]

"The truth is, I was thinking of a fairly big ground surface, and then having the castle stand on that. But that was perhaps pushing it, so in the end, I decided to make the entire thing a building.

"As in drawings one and two, I considered having a castle on the bottom as well, but the bottom ended up being the semisphere with the etherium crystal.

"I drew three because I though it'd be nice to have green on the top."

4 Laputa, castle in the sky (exterior). [Background]

2

ラピュタの みどりの天蓋

3

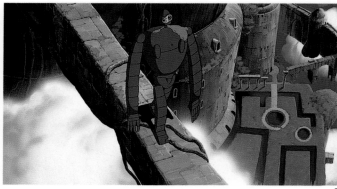

1 Pazu and Sheeta finally arrive at Laputa. [Cel]
2 Robot with different form and role than the robot soldier at Tedus. [Cel]
3 The pair looking down on Laputa from high up. [Cel]
4 The pair arriving in Laputa. [Concept sketch]
5 Garden and castle on Laputa. [Background]

1

1   High-rise residence with balconies and bridges sunk in the water. [Background]
2   Laputa level one (rooftop). [Concept sketch]
3   Laputa level two (town). [Concept sketch]
4   Laputa level three (glass ceiling). [Concept sketch]
5   Laputa level three (residences). [Concept sketch]
6   Pazu and Sheeta surprised at the town of Laputa covered in trees and grasses. [Cel]
7   Minonohashi living in Laputa. [Cel]
    These creatures also appear in Hayao Miyazaki's picture book *The Journey of Shuna* (Animage Bunko). (Primeval mammal species from Tasmania that went extinct in the 17th century [from the storyboard])

151

1

1 Grave marker with a bas-relief of the Laputa royal family crest. [Background]
2 Robots lying down that have become part of the roots of the tree. [Background]
3 Sheeta looking at the enormous tree rising up in the center with emotion. [Cel]
4–5 Robot with a flower plucked to place on the grave. [Cel]
6 Robot and fox-squirrel. [Cel]

3

4

5

2

6

2

3

5

6

4

1   Underside of Laputa. It has crumbled away
    significantly, exposing the interior. [Cel]
2   Laputa (underside). [Cel]
3–4 Wall inside the castle. [Background]
5   Commander and General Muoro searching
    Laputa. [Cel]
6   Pazu and Sheeta after spying on the military.
    [Cel]

1

2

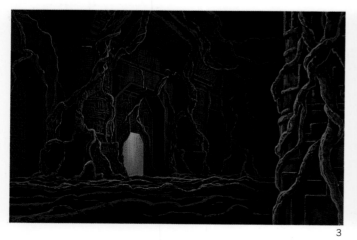

3

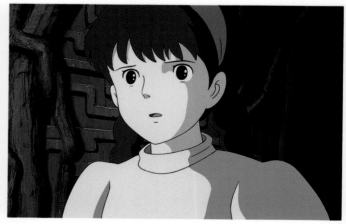

4

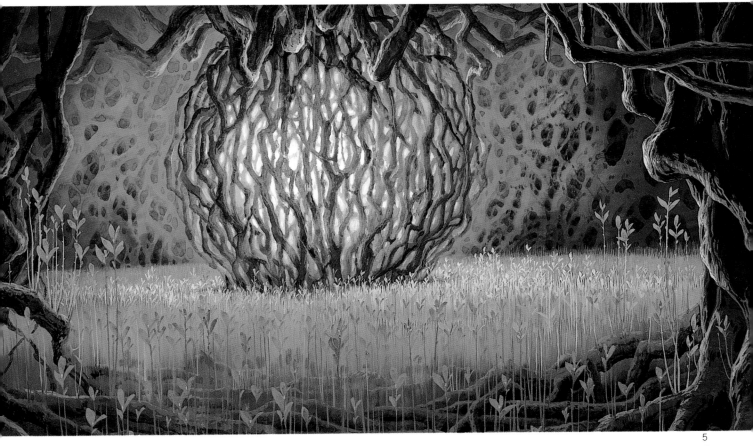

1   Muska and the others inside Laputa's center (within the semisphere). [Film]
2   Laputa's center. [Background]
3   Royal palace covered in tree roots. [Background]
4   Sheeta stunned at the light from the enormous etherium crystal. [Cel]
5   Etherium crystal room. [Background]
6   Muska bathed in the light of the etherium crystal, face filled with madness. [Cel]
7   Black stone tablet. [Background]
8   Enormous etherium crystal. [Film]

1, 6 Pazu hanging on to the tree roots clinging to the
semisphere. [Cel]
2 Mad Muska. [Cel]
3 Semisphere. [Background]
4 Laputa's lightning. [Film]
5 Stone pillars jutting out from the semisphere. [Film]

1

2

Combined double exposure

Holography, one of the products of Laputa's incredible scientific prowess. It's as if the object is there … and it's not. This is the technique we came up with to produce that mysterious sensation. For instance, Muska. To have one picture on-screen, two types of cels were made and combined there. One cel was a fully painted Muska. For the other, a cel with the exact same picture was made but with some parts colored and others not. These materials were each double exposed at 50 percent and combined on the screen. (The actual filming data is not 50 percent each.) So the parts where both were colored show up on the screen as images at 100 percent, while those parts where one was colored and the other wasn't show up as images at 50 percent. And this is how we produced the abnormal sensation of holography.

3

5

6

4

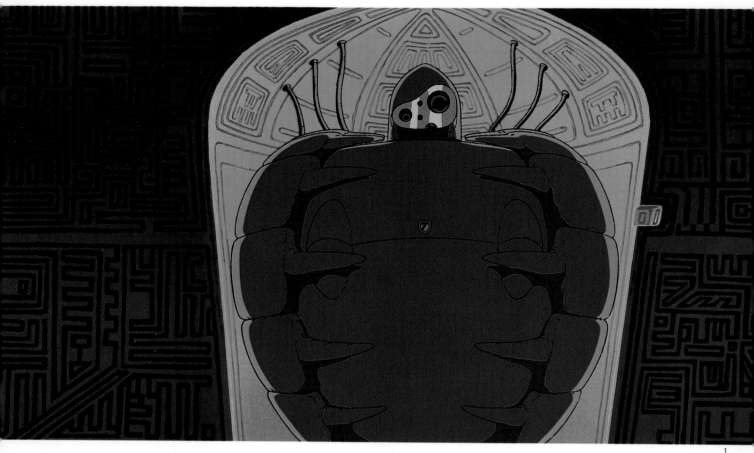

1

2

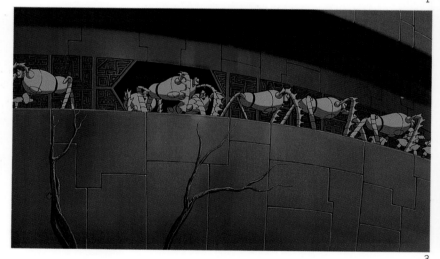

3

1   Robot soldier appearing from the wall in a
    passageway. [Cel]
2   Soldiers under attack by robot soldiers.
    [Concept sketch]
3   Robot soldiers attacking soldiers. [Cel]
4   Group of robots passing by *Tiger Moth*. [Cel]
5   Robot soldiers swarming around *Goliath*.
    [Cel]
6–7 Robot soldiers like pupae in the hangar.
    [Background]
8   Pazu just barely managing to cling to the
    hole the robots were shot from. [Cel]

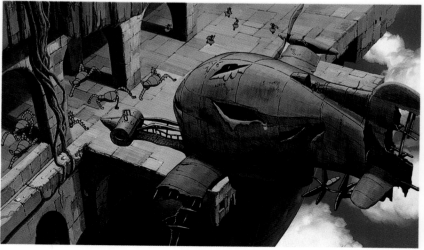

4

5

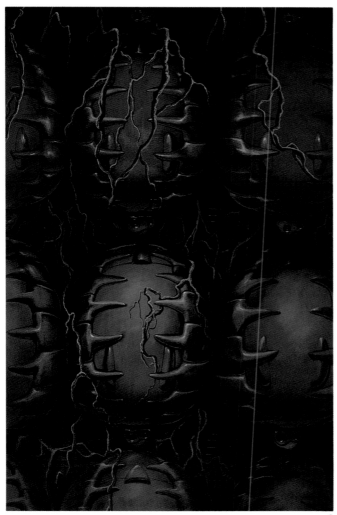

6

7

8

1

2

3

4

5

7

1   *Goliath* projected on the 3-D screen. [Cel]
2   Muska shaking with delight at Laputa's military strength. [Cel]
3   Sheeta fleeing through the robot corridor after Muska has
      taken the etherium crystal from her. [Cel]
4   Robot corridor. [Background]
5   Sheeta and Muska facing off among the thrones. [Cel]
6   The bullets Muska fires cut off Sheeta's braids. [Cel]
7   Muska aiming a gun at Sheeta. [Cel]

6

1

2

3

4

5

6

8

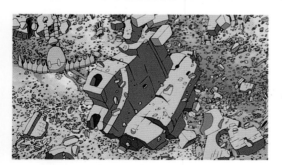

1   Pazu coming into the throne room to save Sheeta. [Cel]
2   Pazu steeling himself to use the spell of destruction. [Cel]
     Pazu: "Sheeta, listen to me very carefully. Whisper the
     spell to me. I'll say it with you."
3   Pazu smiles gently at Sheeta. [Cel]
     Pazu: "Dola and the boys are free. Don't worry about
     them."
4   Sheeta accepting Pazu's idea of shared destruction and
     smiling. [Cel]
5   The pair using the spell of destruction. [Cel]
     Both: "Balus."
6   *Tiger Moth* making an emergency landing on Laputa.
     [Concept sketch]
7   The massive destruction ends midway and Laputa ascends.
     [Film]
8   Dola and the others staring at the ascending Laputa. [Cel]

7

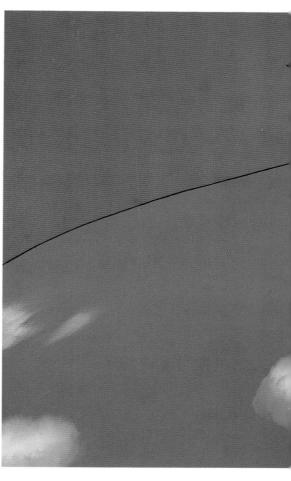

1   The massive tree of Laputa climbing into the sky (pasted over the cutout background on the cel). [Background]
2   Pazu and Sheeta escaping with the kite. [Cel]
3   Pirates showing Pazu and Sheeta the gems they took from Laputa. [Cel]
4   Pazu and Sheeta laughing. [Cel]
5   Sunset sky. [Background]

2

3

4

5

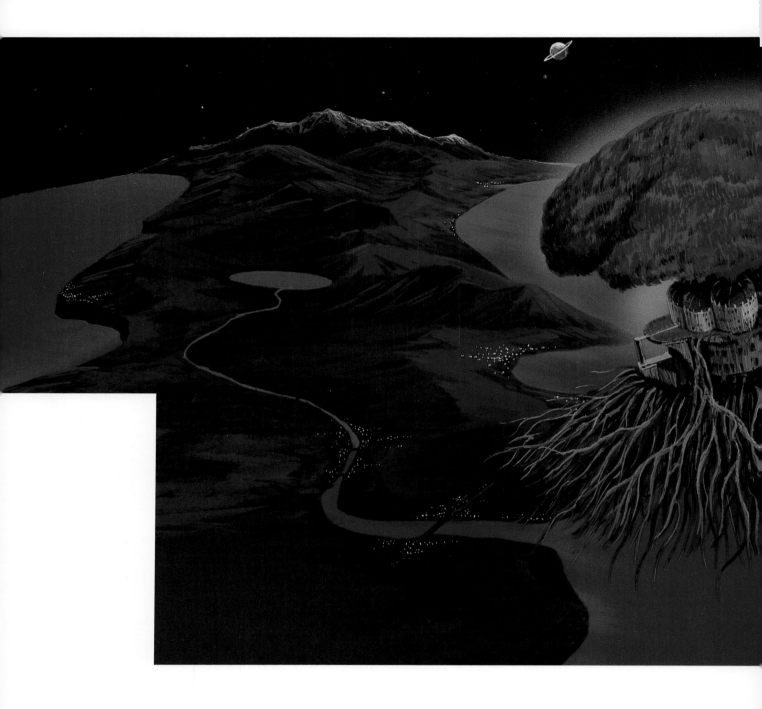

1 Ending. [Cel]
"In the last scene, the giant tree is pulled up by the etherium
crystal and rises into the sky. I was a bit concerned that children
watching it might think that the fox-squirrels and birds would
die if Laputa just kept going into the sky like this. So I thought,
this! This is the ending!

"I was told that it's strange since now we have photos taken
from satellites. But this is a story from before Apollo went into
space, so I insisted that it was fine like this. All the while saying
you could see Laputa from below. [*laughs*]

"If I had had more time, I would've done several other things.
Still, it rains, lightning flashes. Although that's just when
the credits are rolling, so it might be a bit hard to see. I also
considered having a UFO or something come along and bring
Laputa to the ground, but I figured that was too much, so I gave
up on that. [*laughs*] But Nozaki (Toshiro) did draw in a proper
Saturn with rings in the background. [*laughs*]"

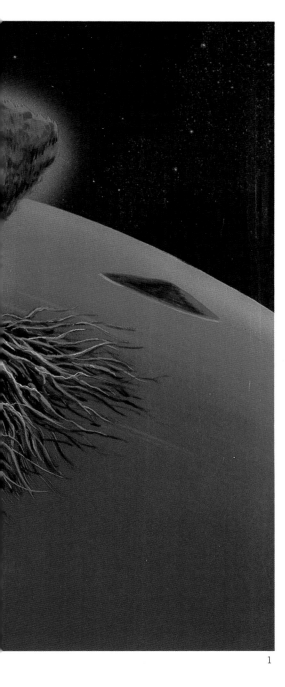

1

170

CASTLE
IN THE SKY

Dub Screenplay

Script: Hayao Miyazaki

The draft screenplay for *Castle in the Sky* was written by director Hayao Miyazaki himself, and the storyboards were created following the initial screenplay draft, but as work progressed a variety of changes were made to the script. The screenplay presented here is the English-language dub script, based on the final Japanese version.

Setting

The time is the period when the science fiction pioneer Jules Verne (1825–1905) was active. However, the exact date and location are not specified. The region is somewhere in Europe. The nation is a constitutional monarchy (but the king does not appear in this story). An era when fighting between great imperial powers thrives, and the military wields great authority. But the machines, vehicles, and weaponry that appear in this work are not constrained by the history of current technology. Although this could also be said about science fiction writers of the latter half of the 19th century, the thinking underpinning the outlook on the nation and the military and the progress of technology is today's. This is most definitely not a work in favor of nostalgia for some halcyon era. This work has nothing to do with the optimistic cultural writings prevalent in the 19th century.

Castle in the Sky is a fantasy story that can be told with "Once upon a time…" —a story with an enormous airship instead of a dragon, an apprentice mechanic instead of a prince, and flaptors (flying devices that flap wings) instead of horses. After coming to the understanding that the world is the earth with limits, this is a story to rehabilitate the extinct "treasure island"—where treasure island is not wealth and riches, but longing and adventure themselves.

What is Laputa?

A model exists for the castle in the sky depicted in the Laputa portion of the third part of Swift's *Gulliver's Travels*. That would be the Laputariches noted in Plato's lost geography *On the Heavens*.

Laputariches was built when a great technological civilization (the current one is the second) thrived, by a people who hated war and fled to the sky. However, at the end of the life of the civilization, which had reached too high an altitude, the Laputians lost their vitality, and the population gradually declined, until they died out due to a strange disease that broke out abruptly around 500 BCE.

Legend has it that some of the Laputians went down to earth, hid themselves and lived on, but the details are unclear.

The Laputian palace became deserted, and the robots continued to protect it, waiting for the return of the king. However, the territory was gradually destroyed over the long years, and now only part of it wanders through the sky. Since the island is always the source of a low-pressure system, it is hidden in the peaks of the clouds, and it moves with the westerlies, so it has never once been seen from the ground.

Now, the theory that there existed a culture that selfishly indulged in nuclear energy before the current technical civilization is even in the modern age espoused by a few people. This is based on the Hindu epics *Ramayana* and *Mahabharata*, and the number of believers in this theory is particularly great in India.

Sea of clouds in the moonlight:

A strange airship flies along, smearing the peaks of the clouds. It is the Tiger Moth, captained by female pirate of the sky, Dola. The watchman at the prow spots a skyliner traveling through the valley in the clouds below. The ship's crew bustles about on the ship before beginning the attack. The door to the hangar opens to spit flaptors out into the sky, a total of four. The winged flying machines known as flaptors, each ridden with two pirates aboard, drop like stones, wings busily flapping, until they catch the air current, brush along the clouds, and charge toward the passenger ship.

Skyliner (passenger ship)

A medium-sized, average ship. A chandelier glitters in an appropriately stylish salon, where passengers are relaxing. Through the salon window, the figure of a girl can be seen in the window of a small room a ways off, the heroine, Sheeta. The look on her face hints at the fact that she is a prisoner. A man in black glasses watches over her, blocking the doorway. Suddenly, a flight of flaptors cuts across the window. At the same time, cries and alarms ring out within the ship.
"Pirates!"
The flight of flaptors approaches the prow of the passenger ship. The pirates launch shot after shot into the control room. An explosion in the control room is followed by yellow powder shooting out of the bullets and scattering all over.
"Blinders!"
The place is in chaos with people pressing their hands over their eyes, people coughing. The pirates glide along the belly of the ship, ascend and land on the main body. Using hooks and ropes, they leap into the cabin on the lower part of the skyliner.

Airship Captain & Airship Crewman #1: Huh?! (Gasp)

Dola: (Laughs) Heee!

Airship Crewman #1: (Ad-lib: Coughing walla)

Airship Crewman #2: Mayday! Mayday! (Coughs)

Airship Crew #3 & #4: (Straining to lift machine gun) Ooh…ah…

Shalulu & Lui: [MNS] (Attack yell)

Pirates 1 &2: (Attack yell)

Shalulu: (To picture) (React to people repeatedly landing on him)

Anli: [MNS] (Insane combat yell)

Dola: (Landing and charging)

2 Airship Crewmen: (Screams)

Airship Crewman: (From last shot) (Screams then) Pirates!

2 Airship Crewmen: (React to hit)

Anli: (War whoop)

Crewman #2: [MNS] (Yells falling down steps)

Passengers: (Intermittent surprised & afraid walla)

Passengers: (Ad-lib: surprised and afraid walla)

Dola: [CMI] (Chuckles)

Dola: (Burst through door effort the react to shooting)

Muska: [MNS] Hold them off!

Muska: [On-Off] Sheeta stay out of the way and you won't get hurt.

Sheeta: (breathing as she prepares to hit Muska over the head. Effort, grunt c/t then c/m as she hits him.)

Men w/ Sunglasses: (React to gun blast)

Sunglasses #1/A: (coughs)

Men with Sunglasses: [OS] (Ad-lib: coughing walla)

Lui: (Wild scream)

Men with Glasses: (Continue coughing and combat walla)

Dola: [OS] (What's wrong?) Hurry up. Break the door down!

Sheeta: (Effort, lifting window)

Sheeta: (Panic breathing and efforts at window. Climbing out window and slipping)

Lui: (breaking in) Oomph!

Shalulu: [MNS] (Pants)

Lui: Where is she?

Lui: Ooh.

Sheeta: (Gasps- struggle/efforts the jumps) No!

Lui: Hey, I found her. She's hidin' out here.

Dola: Don't let her escape. Quick, get her!

Lui: (Straining as he reaches for Sheeta) Come on Sweetheart! Come on sweet…(As he falls) Aw!

Dola: (Effort- grabbing Lui)

Sheeta: (Efforts- struggles to hold on)

Lui: [OS] (Whimpering) Whoa! Mom, don't let me go!

Dola: [OS] Quit your whining. I've got ya.

Dola: (Ah) She's wearing the crystal! Now go get her!

Shalulu: Uh…right!

Sheeta: (Struggle. Efforts.)

Dola: I want that crystal.

Sheeta: (Gasps) [End MNS]

Couple: (Fearful walla)

Sheeta: Uh…(Screams as she falls)

Dola: Oh no, there goes my crystal! Oh no!

Title Sequence

Crowd: (Quiet Street walla)

Crowd: (Faint eating and drinking walla)

Pazu: I need some meatballs for the boss, please.

Shop owner: All right. You sure are working late tonight Pazu.

Pazu: Sigh/You're not kidding. Things are finally busy for a change.

Woman: [MNS] Still working?

Pazu: Yep! Bye!

Pazu: Huh?

Pazu: What is that?

Pazu: [BTC & MNS] (Panting)

Pazu: (Running) It looks like a body.

Pazu: Whoa. (Panting and efforting)

Pazu: (As he almost falls off balance) Huh…Whoa…

Pazu: (Reacting to the light disappearing around Sheeta's pendant) Um?

Pazu: Hmmm.

Pazu: (Reacting to Sheeta getting heavy all of a sudden) Aw!

Pazu: [On MNS] (Ad-lib straining as he struggles to lift Sheeta)

Pazu: (Ad-lib Straining as he carries her over to a platform and sets her down.)

Pazu: (Exhales with relief)

Boss Duffy: [OS] (Calling out) Pazu!

Pazu: (Reacting to Boss) Huh?

Boss Duffy: [On-MNS] What are you doing up there? Did you bring my dinner?

Pazu: [BTC] Ya, I did but…

Pazu: This girl came down from the sky…

Boss Duffy: Errr [MNS] Blast these old pipes! (Ad-lib: straining)

Pazu: (Ad-lib frustrated reactions and grunts as he fetches the pail, returns to Sheeta to cover her up) Here ya go. (Calling out) Boss!

Pazu: Listen Boss, A girl came down…

Boss: (Reacting to pipes)

Boss Duffy: Confound this stupid engine! Just when I get one thing fixed.

Pazu: Listen to me. A girl came down…

Boss Duffy: [OS] Pazu, tighten the second valve, will ya? There's no time to lose. Ah, this machinery's too old.

Pazu: (Efforting)

Pazu: (Straining as he turns valve)

Boss Duffy: (Effort) I think I need a bigger wrench.

Pazu: [MNS] I'll get it.

Boss Duffy: [MNS] Go run the hoist while I fix this.

Pazu: (Shocked, incredulous) Huh?!

Boss: [OS] You think you can do it?

Pazu: (Brightens up) Yeah! Here!

Boss: [OS] Just stay calm and use your head.

Pazu: (Determined) Right!

Pazu: (Seeing Sheeta) Huh?

Boss Duffy: (Alarmed) Hit the brake! Now!

Pazu: What?! Oh!!

Pazu: (Relieved) Phew!

Engineer: [OS-MNS] Well, how'd it go boys?

Miner A: No silver, not even any tin.

Engineer: We're just not having any luck.

Miner B: [MNS] Maybe we would if we tried digging the mines just east of here.

Miner C: I dunno. Those mines are worse than this one.

Miner A: We'll just have to start all over again.

Engineer: (Weary sigh, then) Let's call it a day.

Miner C: Nite.

Miner B: (Sigh)

All miners: (Pushing in unison)

Boss: [MNS-on] (Calling out to Pazu) Shut off the boiler, Pazu. We're not going to find anything today.

Pazu: But… (Small sigh)

Boss: [OS] (Bitterly, more to himself) If things keep going like this, we'll all be starving soon.

Boss Duffy: [OS] (Calling out) And Pazu! Maybe you can oil that blasted machine.

Pazu: (Calling out) 'Kay!

Boss: Thanks. Good night.

Pazu: Nite!

Shalulu: (Slightly whimpering) Mom it's no use, let's call it off. There's too much cloud cover. It's too dark. (Dola reacts)

Dola: (P.O'd sound) What!

Shalulu: Mom, don't worry, I'll find her.

Dola: [MNS] We'll all find her.

Pazu: (Running around noises)

Pazu: (Yawning and Stretching)

Pigeons: Coo

Sheeta: (Gasps)

Sheeta: [MNS] (Turning)

Pazu: [OS] (Cheerful laughter, then) Hello. It's about time you got up! Oh. (Off birds)

Pazu: [OS] (Through laughter to birds) How're you feeling?

Sheeta: (Giggle)

Pazu: (Coming down the roof, to Sheeta) Hi there! (Shaking her hand) My name's Pazu. I'm really glad to see you're doing all right. You had me worried there.

Pazu: [OS] Go ahead, feed 'em. Don't be shy. These guys are really happy we have a visitor.

Sheeta: [On-off] (Ad-lib: Reaction and giggling as pigeons swarm on her)

Pazu: Well thank goodness, you laugh like a regular person. The way you fell from the sky, I thought that maybe you were an angel or something.

Sheeta: Thank you very much for saving me. Oh I'm so sorry, my name is Sheeta.

Pazu: Sheeta. What a beautiful name. Ya, I had to catch you, you were just floating and I…

Sheeta: Oh really. Well I remember an airship, but I can't remember anything else.

Pazu: [HIS BTC] You're sure that's all you remember?

Sheeta: (Nodding in agreement) Uh-hm. [Continues MNS] I'm not sure how I survived.

Pazu: (Bending over to put pigeons down) Well I think I might have an idea about that.

Pazu: May I see your necklace for a second?

Sheeta: This?

Sheeta: [OS] My grandmother gave it to me. It's been in my family for generations.

Pazu: Wow! It's beautiful.

Pazu: Could you hold this?

Pazu: (Ad-lib: Grunts as he tries to fasten necklace around his own neck)

Pazu: (After Sheeta helps) Oh.

Pazu: Thanks!

Pazu: (Turning) Heh-heh-heh!

Pazu: [Off-on] Get a load of this!

Pazu: Ready. Watch! (Jumping) Here I goooooo!

Sheeta: Huh? Ah!

Sheeta: (Small breaths)

Sheeta: [MNS] (Ad-lib small grunts as she jumps off the end of the roof)

Pazu: (Grunts as he climbs up.)

Pazu: (Sheepish chuckle)

Pazu: Hmm. Well so maybe I had the wrong idea about your necklace.

Pazu: (Falling again) Aaahhhh!

Sheeta: [On-MNS] (Reacting) Ah!...oh…

Pazu: [On-Off] (Groaning and straining)

Sheeta: (Ad-lib straining trying to climb down)

Sheeta: [On-Off] (Screams as she falls)

Pazu: (Reacting to Sheeta falling) Whoa!

Pazu: (As Sheeta lands on him) Ugh! (Moans)

Sheeta: Ahh…

Pazu: (Groans)

Sheeta: I'm so sorry Pazu!

Pazu: Uh…ah...

Sheeta: Are you okay?

Pazu: I'm fine.

Sheeta: Oh, you scared me. Does it hurt much?

Pazu: (If quick can finish on-screen) Are you kidding?! If my head were any harder you could use it as a cannonball. [Finishes OS]

Sheeta: (Giggles)

Sheeta & Pazu: (Laughs)

Sheeta: (Laughs)

Pazu: (Suddenly interrupts laugh, panic-stricken) Whoa, the kettle! Must be boiling over. Come on, let's go. Follow me. This way.

Pazu: (On-Off) I'll get breakfast started. You can wash up over there.

Pazu: (His back to camera) There's a clean towel too.

Sheeta: Oh, thank you.

Sheeta: (To herself, awed) Laputa…

Pazu: (Calling out) Sheeta! It's time for breakfast.

Pazu: (Mouth not shown in middle) My father took that picture from an airship. He loved to fly.

Pazu: [OS] It's Laputa. A floating island.

Sheeta: (Awed) An island that floats in the sky?

Pazu: Yup. Most people think it's just a legend.

Pazu: [OS] (Eagerly) But my dad actually saw it. That's a picture of his airship.

Pazu: [OS] It looked like a castle just floating there in the sky. He said it was the most amazing thing he'd ever seen.

Pazu: And that's the only picture he was able to take.

Pazu: But take a look at this Sheeta. Dad kept a journal and he made all sorts of drawings of Laputa. See?

Pazu: [OS] There it is. And he drew the castle and also what he though the people looked like. He was sure the castle was filled with treasure. But nobody believed him. They called him a liar.

Pazu: (Sad and bitter) Being called a liar is what killed him.

Pazu: (Cheering up, running toward the plane) But I am going to prove that my dad was no liar, Sheeta.

Pazu: As soon as I'm done building this plane—I'm gonna take off and find Laputa myself.

Pazu: (Reacting to car) Huh?

Dola: Hmm.

Sheeta: (Gasps)

Pazu: Wow, it's a real automobile! You don't see many of those around here.

Sheeta: (Serious, low voice) Those people are pirates, Pazu.

Pazu: (Shocked) Huh?

Sheeta: [OS] They're the ones who attacked the airship.

Pazu: Then they're probably after you!

Sheeta: (Gasps)

Pazu: (Urgent) Come on.

Sheeta: [MNS] (Reacting) Uh…

Lui: [On-Off] Hey, whoa, hold on. Wait up, wait up, wait up, wait up, wait up.

Pazu: Ah yes. How can I help you mister?

Lui: Young man, query? Have you seen a little girl around here?

Pazu: Huh, let me see now. Yeah, there're about a hundred little girls in this town. Which one?

Lui: (Frustrated grunt)

Lui: Thanks for nothin' kid!

Pazu: Sure. Bye.

Pazu: (Whispering, tense) They are definitely after you, Sheeta.

Pirate C: Lui, go tell your mother, she's in disguise.

Lui: So she's in disguise. Go tell my mother. [Ends MNS]

Pirate C: (Slow burn)

Boss Duffy: Haven't seen her.

Shalulu: That's what you keep saying, but I want you to really think hard about it.

Pazu: [MNS] (Calling out, urgent) Boss!

Pazu: [MNS] (Shouting as he runs) Boss!

Pazu & Sheeta: (Ad-lib: Panting)

Shalulu: She'd be about the age of those two.

Pazu & Sheeta: (More panting)

Sheeta: (trips)…Ah…oh…

Shalulu & Anli: (Reacting to Sheeta) Huh?! Huh?

Sheeta: Uh…(Pants)

Lui: [OS] There she is! Don't let her get away!

Lui: Grab her!!

Shalulu & Anli: (Attacking) Now!

Pazu & Sheeta: (Ad-lib grunts as they duck and slide)

Pazu: Boss, they're pirates. They're after her.

Shalulu & Anli: (Ad-lib grunts as they get up)

Madge: (Excited) Pirates! (As she gets pulled inside, fretting) I want to see, wahhhh!

Sheeta: (Being yanked inside, surprised) Aw!

Boss Duffy: You can stop right there my friend.

Shalulu: Think you're tough. Don't ya?

Boss Duffy: (Sarcastic) I'm tough enough!

Lui: (Proudly) We'll see about that!

Boss Duffy: [MNS] Just go away! We're honest folks here.

Pazu: (Being yanked OS) Whoa…

Pazu: Hey wait, what'd you do that for?

175

Boss's Wife: (Urgent) Quick, leave from the back!

Pazu: (Defiant) I'm gonna fight 'em!

Boss's Wife: (Scolding) Pazu, what if you end up getting yourself hurt?

Pazu: (Challenging) So?

Boss's Wife: (Softening, gently) So somebody's got to protect your friend.

Pazu: Hm? (nodding) Oh! Uh-hm.

Shalulu: Why don't you get out of our way.

Boss Duffy: Why don't you just try and make me?

Shalulu: Maybe I will!

Anli: Oh ya—(Oh ya uh-huh)

Anli: You do it Shalulu.

Shalulu: [On-Off] (Ad-lib: Straining and flexing with action)

Boss Duffy: Hmm…

Townsfolk: (Walla as they urge Duffy to show off his muscles)

Townsman #1: Hey Boss. Show 'em what you're made of!

Boss Duffy: (Ad-lib deep breath and strains with action)

Crowd: (Ad-lib cheering and applauding) Great! That's right! You show 'em Boss. That's it! Hooray. (Etc.)

Shalulu: (Grunt of astonishment)

Lui & Anli: (Ad-lib to mouth moves) Ahh!

Boss Duffy: (Snickers)

Boss's Wife: (Sarcastic) I hope you know I am not mending that.

Boss Duffy: (Deflated) Huh?

Boss's Wife: [CM] Eh-huh.

Shalulu: (Ad-lib grunts and chuckles with action)

Lui: (OS) Take that, you land lover.

Anli: (OS) Well, he took it.

Lui: (OS) He certainly did.

Boss Duffy: (Ad-lib grunts, exhales and chuckles with action)
Anli: (Off-On) Uh haa! Uh haa! That's right!

Lui: (MNS) Come on Shalulu— You're not so big for nothing Shalulu—Yes!

Shalulu: (Ad-lib grunts and chuckles with action)

Boss Duffy: Ugh… Argh…

Townsfolk: (Ad-lib grunts and cheers as they catch boss then cheer on "Come on!" Etc.)

Shalulu: Ugh…

Anli & Lui: Ooo. He said mom was ugly—now go get him!

Shalulu: (OM, CT) Huh?!! (Growl)

Townsfolk: (Ad-lib: Cheering walla)

Shalulu & Boss: (Ad-lib: Fighting walla) I'll give you ugly. (Etc.)

Townsfolk Lui & Anli: (Cheering walla: That's it, get him. Come on, get him! Show him! etc.)

Anli: (Excited, happy) Yeah, you got him. Yesss.

Townsman #2: [OS] Hey Loudmouth!

Anli: (Reacting to Townsman #2) No. (Hit) Ugh!!

Lui: (Reacts to Anli) Yea! Ooo get in there. Give him a left! Give him a right!

Townsfolk: (Cheering walla)

Townsfolk: (Brawling walla)

Lui: (Brawling walla) You dog! Ruffian! Rogue! Vile, vile, vile!

Dola: Whoa.

Dola: They're headed for the railroad tracks. Let's move it!

Sheeta & Pazu: (Panting)

Sheeta: (Grunts)

Pazu: (Hailing the train) Heeey! Hey! Hey!

Pazu: (To Sheeta) (Off-On) We're gonna jump on, Sheeta!

Sheeta: (Ad-lib straining & running) Right!

Pazu: [OS] That's it.

Sheeta: Come on.

Pazu: Um!

Engine Man: Hey Pazu, who's your friend there?

Sheeta: (Ad-lib: Climbing up effort)

Pazu: Her name is Sheeta (Then mouth behind arm pointing) Pirates are after us!

Engine Man: Huh?

Pazu: It's the Dola gang!

Engine man: I'll be, pirates!

Pazu: Can you drop us off at the police in the next town?

Engine man: Sure, ah tell you what. Help me stoke up the engine!

Pazu: [MNS] Will do!

Townsfolk: (Excited walla)

Lui: Uh?

Lui: (Delighted, surprised) Hey, it's mom!

Townsfolk: (Panic walla)

Dola: You chowder heads! Get your brother and hop on!

Lui: Huh? But Sheeta's hiding inside that house.

Dola: Lame brain, they made an escape!

Dola: Now step on it!

Lui: They escaped?!

Anli: Hey, I wanna come.

Shalulu: Aargh… mommy...

Shalulu: Ow… eh…

Townsfolk: (Angry walla as Dola gang gets away) (Reacting to grenade, running away) Whoa!

Pazu: (Ad-lib: Strains/grunts as he stokes engine)

Engine man: Hey, Pazu, here they come!

Pazu: Hey, Can't this engine go any faster?

Engine man: This is the best she'll do. She's old.

Pirate (Patch): (Reacting to almost being knocked out of car)

Dola: Floor it. (taking over the wheel) Move over.

Shalulu, Anli, Lui, 2 pirates: (Various ad-lib panic and fearful walla)

Shalulu, Anli, Lui, 2 pirates: (Continue walla)

Pirate B: (Reacting) Whoa!

Pirates: (Ad-lib: Yelling as they chase the train)

Lui: (With vibration) (Ah) I'd really prefer to be in the car mother.

Engine man: Increase the steam!

They're gaining on us!

Shalulu: We got 'em (Ma).

Dola: (Ferocious victory noises)

Pazu: (To Sheeta) We need you in here.

Pazu: Help with the fire!

Sheeta: (Mouth not shown) Okay!

Pazu: (partially OS) (straining as he tries to unfasten coupling)

Pazu: (Straining as he separates the cars)

Shalulu, Anli, Lui, 2 Pirates: (Reacts to impact)

Dola: (Jumps—Regains balance) Charge!

Pazu: (Ad-lib yelling)

Pazu: (Ad-lib grunts)

Dola: Come on kiddies! Get 'em! Get 'em!

Shalulu & Lui: (Efforting through cars)

Pazu: (Grunts)

Pazu: (Effort)

Lui: (Impact noise)

Dola: Hey come back here. Stooooooop!

Dola: You'll get yours!

Dola: Don't just stand there. Push this train over the cliff.

Shalulu & Lui: Woozy noises.

Shalulu & Lui: (Dismayed) What?

Engine man: (His back to camera) (Laughs, then) We sure showed them!

Pazu: (Efforting)

Pazu: (To Sheeta) I can do it now.

Sheeta: No, I can do it.

Dola: Heave, heave, heave!
Shalulu: (Effort, effort, effort)
Anli: And heave, and heave, and heave, and stop.
Lui: (Effort, effort, effort)

Dola: (Alarmed, sharply) wait.

Lui: (Awed, fearful) Ah, you think maybe it's Muska?

Dola: Ya, it's Muska all right. We got to find those kids.

Engine man: Huh?!

Engine man: Well whatta you know about that. It's the army to the rescue.

Engine man: (Calling out) Heeey! Could you kindly help these two young people? Pirates have been chasing them all day!

Sheeta: (Gasps, reacting to the man with dark glasses)

Pazu: (Low) Huh? (turns) What's a matter? (As she runs away) Huh? (Efforts- trips evil guy)

Sheeta: [On-Off] (Whimper of fear) Goodbye, Pazu.

Pazu: Huh?

Sunglasses #1: (Calling out) Young Lady, come back here! (Pants and grunts)

Sunglasses #1: (as they trip) Ugh!

Officer #2: (As he trips) Aw!

Pazu: (As he almost loses balance) Ugh!

Officer: (As he falls) Whoa!

Pazu: [OS] (Struggling with the officer, calling out) Sheeta! Wait!

Officer: Halt! Or I'll shoot!

Engine man: (Efforting)

Sunglasses #1: (Grunts/screams)

Sheeta: (Panting as she runs)

Lui: (Warning, scared) That's an armored train, mother!

Dola: And we're the Dola gang. Attack!

Sheeta: (Gasps, runs off)

Pazu: Oh no! (Sheeta turns and starts to run) Hey!

Pazu: [Mouth not shown] Wait! Sheeta!

Sheeta: Don't follow me! [MNS] You'll get hurt.

Pazu: Ah…ugh!

Shalulu, Anli, Lui: (Ad-lib: frightened walla)

Shalulu, Anli, Lui: Whooooaa!

Pazu: (Reacts to Dola's oncoming train)

Pirates (Dola's boys): (Ad-lib reaction through rest of sequence)

Sheeta: (Check for running walla through sequence)

Pazu: (Grunts as he grabs Sheeta then leaps)

Sheeta: Ah!

Pazu & Sheeta: (Cry out and grunt)

Pazu: (Straining)

Sheeta: Don't let go!

Dola & the boys: (yell and impact)

Dola: [MNS] (Rolls into frame efforts—then out) Come on!

Shalulu: (Efforts)

Lui: [Off-On] Where are they mother?

Dola: Be quiet! Just watch them.

Pazu & Sheeta: (Ad-lib struggle & strain)

Pazu & Sheeta: (Scream as they fall)

Shalulu: (To pic. Fear)

Dola: Huh?

Dola: (Coarse inhale, then delighted) Ahhhh!!

Pazu & Sheeta: (Surprised reaction)

Pazu: (Amazed) Sheeta, we're floating!

Sheeta: Ah…uhh…

Pazu: You see, this is what happened the first time I saw you.

Dola: (Excited) See that? It's the power of the crystal!

Pazu: I knew it. I knew there was something special about your necklace.

Sheeta: (Gasps as he lets one hand go)

Pazu: (Laughs at her fears)

Sheeta: (Ad-lib slight noise, first puzzled then happy/amazed)

Pazu: The necklace will let us down nice and easy.

Dola: Boys, I want that crystal!

Soldier: (Officer) [OS] Fire!

Pirates (All): (Ad-lib: Panicky walla)

Dola: It's fantastic! Incredible!

Dola: [Mouth not shown] [Her BTC] I must have that crystal!

Pirates, Lui, Anli: (Frightened walla, running) Whoa!

Sheeta: [OS] It's going out!

Pazu: Ah wait just a minute!

Pazu: I guess your necklace must come to life whenever you're in trouble.

Pazu: [OS] Wow. That's a long way up.

Sheeta: I hope they're all right, your boss and his wife and that nice train engineer.

Pazu: My friends are all miners. They can take care of themselves. I wouldn't worry about them if I were you. Come on Sheeta. Let's go.

Pazu: This has been a mining town as long as anyone can remember; most of these tunnels aren't even used any more.

Pazu: [OS] Here ya go.

Sheeta: Thank you.

Sheeta: [Mouth not shown] I'm glad you brought some food. I'm starving.

Pazu: And for dessert, I've got a green apple and some candy.

Sheeta: Really?

Sheeta: Is that bag of yours magic or something?

Sheeta: [OS] It's always got just what we need.

Pazu: (Poss. "Yup" or affirm sound)

Sheeta: (Giggles then quietly eats)

Pazu: Sheeta, where exactly do you come from?

Sheeta: I come from Gondoa, deep in the northern mountains. I used to live there with my parents and we were very happy.

Sheeta: [VO] But when my mother and father died, I was all alone. The only thing that kept me going was the farm and taking care of my animals. But one day, everything changed. That was the day the men came and took me away.

Pazu: Whoa wait a minute. You mean they kidnapped you?

Sheeta: Yes.

Pazu: It was that man in the dark glasses…

Sheeta: Uh hm.

Pazu: (Thoughtful) I wonder who that guy is and what he is doing with the army.

Pazu: (Bites/munches apple) You know what I think. I think, Dola and that man are both after your necklace.

Sheeta: Well, Pazu, I had no idea that this crystal was so incredibly powerful.

Sheeta: It's been in my family as long as I can remember. Mother gave it to me before she died and she told me never to show it or give it away to anyone.

Pazu: (Assessing—trying to put it together) Huhm…(Munches apple)

Pazu: Well we orphans should stick together, don't you think.?

Sheeta: I'm really sorry. It's my fault getting you mixed up on all this.

Pazu: Are you kidding? This is the most exciting thing that's ever happened to me. I wouldn't miss an adventure like this for anything in the world.

Sheeta: Really?

Pazu: (Startled noise)

Sheeta: (Gasp)

Uncle Pom: Are you some sort of goblin, come to torment men?

Pazu: (Delighted, calling out) It's Uncle Pom!

(To Sheeta: Don't worry, he's a friend.

[On-Off] (Calling out again) Uncle Pom!

Pazu: Uncle Pom! Boy am I glad to see you.

Uncle Pom: I can't see you clearly yet goblin, but you sound like Pazu. (Looks to Sheeta) and if these old eyes don't deceive me, there's a she-goblin with you.

Pazu: There are pirates chasing us, Uncle Pom.

Uncle Pom: Oh!?

Pazu: And the army's right behind them.

Uncle Pom: (Chuckles) That sounds absolutely splendid!

Uncle Pom: (His back to the camera) The tea is ready, help yourself.

Sheeta: Thank you. This is great.

Sheeta: Don't you get lonely down here underground, Uncle Pom?

Uncle Pom: (Chuckles) Never, my dear. All of these rocks are my friends and they often talk to me. Ever since last night they've been especially restless.

Pazu: (Sips, OWS, blows on his tea)

Pazu: (Puzzled) The rocks talk to you?

Uncle Pom: [OS] Oh yes, Pazu, the earth speaks to all of us and if we listen, we can understand.

Uncle Pom: (Chuckles) The rocks speak in a very small voice. (Blows out light)

Sheeta: Huh?!

Sheeta: (Slight gasp, reacting to crystal glowing) Oh my!

Pazu: (Amazed) Whoa.

Pazu: (Awed) Amazing!

Sheeta: Pazu! Look above us!

Pazu: Huh?! Wow!

Pazu: It was just a hunk of rock a while ago.

Sheeta: Oh my.

Uncle Pom: The answer lies inside these rocks. Let me show you.

Sheeta & Pazu: [OS] Wow!

Uncle Pom: [OS] It's a long-forgotten element called "Aetherium."

Sheeta: Pazu, you see?

Uncle Pom: All the rocks around here contain a bit of Aetherium.

Pazu: Really?

Uncle Pom: [OS] Our kind once knew how to mine Aetherium, but no longer.

Sheeta: (Reacting to crystal) Wait.

Sheeta: Look, my stone's glowing.

Uncle Pom: (Shocked) Well goodness. Bless my soul. That's a pure aetherium crystal!

Uncle Pom: [OS] (Awed) There hasn't been one since before my great grandfather's time!

Uncle Pom: No wonder the rocks were restless.

Sheeta: This stone possesses incredible power.

Uncle Pom: Legend has it that only the people of the floating city of Laputa knew how to make such crystals.

Sheeta: They made this crystal?

Uncle Pom: They used Aetherium to make Laputa float in the sky.

Pazu: (excited) I knew Laputa wasn't just made up. You see Sheeta? It's just like my dad said.

Uncle Pom: (Trembling)

Pazu: What's the matter?

Uncle Pom: [On-Off] (Trembling) I'm sorry, but would you put that crystal away? It's too strong for me.

Sheeta: (Puzzled, but eager to oblige) Oh, sorry.

Pazu: What is it, Uncle Pom?

Uncle Pom: (Big sigh)

Uncle Pom: Great Grandpa used to tell me— (long shot) That the rocks become restless when Laputa appears over the mine.

Pazu: (Excited) Wow, so that must mean Laputa's over the mine right now. Listen—

Pazu: Sheeta, now I can prove that the legend is true!

Uncle Pom: Sheeta, I must tell you something.

Sheeta: [MNS] What is it?

Uncle Pom: [On-End] That Crystal is extremely powerful, but with a power that rightfully belongs to the earth from which it came. To forget that, and then to try to use the crystal's power for selfish reasons will bring great unhappiness. You understand?

Sheeta: Yes.

Uncle Pom: Your crystal (should) remind us that we come from the earth and to the earth we must return.

Pazu: Come on, lighten up! Two times already that crystal's gotten Sheeta out of some really big trouble.

Pazu: And I have a feeling that Crystal's going to help us find Laputa.

Lui: It's flying away.

Anli: Mom, can we go back to the ship now please?

Dola: It's too quiet. We'd better just stay put for the time being.

Shalulu: Does this mean no lunch?

Pazu: Coast is clear. Let's go.

Sheeta: [On—mouth not shown] Uncle Pom, thank you!

Uncle Pom: [MNS] Be careful, my dear.

Pazu: (Panting)

Pazu: Wow! Look up there!

Pazu: Beyond that cloud is a floating city that no one here on earth believes exists.

Pazu: (OM CT exertion) But I swear, I am gonna be the one to prove it.

Sheeta: (Hesitant) Pazu?

Pazu: Huh?

Sheeta: Listen, There's something that I haven't told you yet.

Sheeta: You see, my family has a very old traditional name and when the stone was passed on to me.

[OS] I inherited that name.

Sheeta: [On-Off] And the name I inherited was Lusheeta Toel Ul Laputa.

Pazu: (Shocked) Laputa!? You mean you're…(Sees plane) (Gasp)

Pazu: (Alarmed, urgent) They found us, Sheeta—Let's go!

Sheeta: (Panting)

Pazu: [BTC] (Panting) Head back to the mine! Hurry!

Sheeta: (Ad-lib noise as she slides down) (Gasp of horror as soldiers block her way)

Pazu: (Ad-lib noise as he slides down)

Soldier: Hands up!

Pazu: Don't you touch her!

Pazu: (As he is hit) Ugh!

Sheeta: (Screams)

Sheeta: (Ad-lib reaction & struggling as she's grabbed- then biting arm) Let me go!

Sunglasses: (Ad-lib: Yells)

Sheeta: (Desperately calling out) Oh no, are you all right Pazu? You have to wake up Pazu!

Officer: We've captured them!

Muska: (Coldly) And about time.

Pazu: (Ad-lib moans as he stirs, awakens, and tries to get up) (Ad-lib noise as he looks around, gets up, runs and stumbles) Open up! Let me out! (Bashes)

Pazu: (Shouting) Hey. Let me out! (Throwing himself against the door) Ugh! Ugh!

Pazu: Where Am I?

Pazu: (Ad-lib grunts as he climbs up to the window)

Soldier #1: [OS] Forward… March!

Pazu: [On-Off] (Ad-lib: Straining as he struggles to free his head, then it pops free) Ugh! (Falling) Whoa!

General: We're wasting time.

General: You twist an arm or two and I guarantee the girl will talk.

Muska: (Coldly) I respectfully disagree.

Muska: Such "military" tactics risk wasting more time, general.

General: If my military tactics had been used to begin with— Dola wouldn't have had a chance to interfere with us at all!

Muska: It was a military transmission that the pirates decoded.

General: (Indignant) Huh?!

Muska: [OS] You've bungled things sir and now I must fix them.

Muska: Your job, general, is to mobilize the troops when it becomes necessary.

General: Ugh… (Fuming with anger) Muska. Just don't forget that the government put me in charge of finding Laputa.

Muska: Don't forget that as the government's secret agent, I am in charge of you, general.

General: (Fuming) Blast! I really hate that man!

Sheeta: Huh?

Muska: [On-Off] I trust you slept well?

Sheeta: Where is Pazu? Is he all right? I want to see him!

Muska: Now this is fit for a princess.

Muska: Don't worry Sheeta. Your friend is being treated as if he were the guest of royalty.

Muska: I want you to see something before you see him.

Muska: Please step inside.

Sheeta: (Gasps as she sees the robot)

Sheeta: (Fearful) What is it?

Muska: An artificial life-form. It's called a robot. Laputa was just a legend until this dropped from the sky.

Farmer: Uh… Whoa!

Farmer's Wife: (Ad-lib panic)

Muska: (Long shot) Now the government wants me to unlock Laputa's secrets…for example, what's this fellow made of, metal or ceramics? With our limited technology, we have no idea. But he does tell us one thing.

Muska: Come and see… (Reacting to her hesitation) Oh, don't be afraid, Sheeta, he's really quite dead, you know.

Muska: Look there!

Sheeta: (Gasps)

Muska: It's the same emblem that decorates the fireplace in your home—

Muska: —And your crystal.

Muska: [OS] You see, Sheeta, this crystal also comes from Laputa.

Sheeta: (Sobs) [Off-On] And I believe that the powers locked inside it are capable of leading a person back to that city's treasures.

Sheeta: (Exploding) Then why? Why don't you just take it?

Sheeta: [Mouth not shown] (Hands over face, crying) Just take it and keep Laputa's treasures for yourself. But leave Pazu and me alone, please!

Muska: …You think I'm doing this for money? You understand nothing! According to the legend—

Muska: (Intensely) —The same technology that kept Laputa airborne also made it a major power that once dominated the entire planet.

Muska: [Off-On] If such a horrible thing is still floating up there, you can understand what a threat it is to the peace of the world, (As he turns—imploring) Sheeta.

Muska: This stone only works for you. You must know of some way to make the stone point out the location of Laputa.

Sheeta: (Hands over face, desperately) I really don't know anything. Please let me see Pazu!

Muska: I don't want to see any harm come to anyone, but I simply can't control what the military might do to him.

Sheeta: (Big gasp!) What!

Muska: In the event that you cooperate, I'm sure whoever's in charge will grant Pazu his freedom, Lusheeta —

Sheeta: (Gasp)

Muska: [OS] Toel Ul Laputa!

Sheeta: (Slight gasp) You know my real name!

Muska: "Ul" means "ruler" in Laputian. "Toel" means "true." You are the legitimate heir to the throne of Laputa, princess Lusheeta.

Pazu: (Ad-lib: Grunts as he climbs)

Pazu: [On-Off] (As he falls) Whoa!

Pazu: (As he lands) Ugh!

Pazu: (Moans)

Soldier: [OS] Let's go. Out!

Pazu: Uh!?

Pazu: (delighted, calling out) Sheeta!

Sheeta: Are you all right, Pazu?

Pazu: I'm okay, but what about you? They didn't hurt you, did they?

Muska: Pazu, I'm so sorry, there has been a grave misunderstanding.

Muska: [MNS] We had no idea how nobly you fought [On]—to protect our little Sheeta from those awful pirates.

Pazu: What's he talking about?

Sheeta: Pazu, do this for me. Forget about Laputa.

Pazu: What are you saying?

Muska: It's been decided that the search for Laputa will be made secretly by the army with Sheeta's cooperation.

Muska: Really, the best thing you can do is forget you ever heard of the place.

Pazu: (To Sheeta, incredulous) Forget about Laputa?

Sheeta: (Almost in tears) I'm sorry I caused you so much trouble. I hope someday you can forgive me.

Pazu: I can't forget! No way!

Pazu: [OS] Laputa means too much to both of us.

Sheeta: (Turning her back to Pazu, in tears) Goodbye.

Pazu: Sheeta!

Pazu: (Desperately calling after Sheeta, struggling) Come back! Come back!

Muska: Now behave, little boy. Use your head!

Pazu: (Frustrated sigh)

Muska: [On-Off] Here, take this, a little something to show our appreciation of your efforts.

Muska: Only you can do it. Remember the words that bring the crystal to life.

Muska: (Leaning over) Keep your promise and you too will be free.

Sheeta: [Mouth not shown] (Sobbing)

Madge (boss's daughter): Oooh/ (Turns sees Pazu) huh?

Madge (boss's daughter): (Calling her mother OS, excited) Hey, Mommy, Mommy! It's Pazu! Pazu's outside!

Boss's Wife: [On—Off] Oh, my, Pazu! / Well where have you been? We were all very worried about you, Pazu.

Boss's Wife: [OS] What happened to your friend?

Pazu: (Sad/resigned/empty, almost to himself) It's over now.

Boss's Wife: [OS] (Puzzled) What?

Boss's Wife: (Calling after Pazu) Pazu, come back!

Pazu: (Running and panting)

Pazu: (Ad-lib: Grunts as he trips and falls)

Pazu: (Ad-lib: Effort as he lifts coins to throw them away, hesitates)

Pazu: (Weeps)

Pazu: (As he's yanked inside) Whoa!

Pazu: (Ad-lib: Struggling)

Dola: Welcome home sonny! (Takes a big bite)

Pazu: (His back to camera) (Struggling) Get out! Get out or I'll throw you out!

Pazu: (Struggling) This is my house!

Dola: (Teasing) You don't scare me. You can't even protect one small girl.

Pazu: What do you mean?!

Anli: Hey mom, can I keep this money?

Dola: (Munching) Up and sold the little girl, did ya? I know your type.

Pazu: (His back to camera) (Defiant) You don't know what you're talking about.

180

Dola: (Munching) They offered ya money and you took it, didn't ya?

Pazu: (Pained) I only left because Sheeta told me to…(Devastated) that's why.

Dola: (Spits out shell) So you believed her and ya came back here, right? (Challengingly) You're just a scared little boy who runs away.

Pazu: Says you. You don't even have the guts to stand up to Muska and the army.

Dola: He who turns (Quickish) and runs away can steal the treasure another day.

Lui: (Affirm humming) Glug-glug-glug. (Burp) Pardon me.

Shalulu: (Affirm humming)

Dola: (But) Don't you think it's kinda strange that the army has gotten into the kidnapping business? (Bites ham and munches)

Dola: (Lip smack, then) Do you really think they'll keep her alive? [Cont. OS] Don't ya see that they forced her to make a deal?

Pazu: (Helpless) Huh?

Dola: (Chewing ham, talking with mouth full) She saved your life. (Then ad-lib to flaps) Get it now, sonny?

Lui: [OS] (Genuine admiration in his voice) Mother, you amaze me. How do you know these things?

Dola: [OS] Oh well. You can't be a sensitive woman like me without learnin' a few things! Sheeta and I are exactly alike. All warm and mushy and sensitive. (Burp)

Dola: Now so when you boys get married, you go find a gal like her.

Lui: Huh?

Dola: (chugging down wine) Glug-glug.

Lui: (Shocked) Huh? She's gonna end up like mama.

Shalulu: (Ad-lib reaction and grumbling) I didn't get any ham. Give me that.

Lui: Ooh. Ma that was some good food.

Dola: (Concentrating, smiles) Hmm…It won't work changing the code on me. They're calling for air destroyer *Goliath*.

Dola: (alarmed) They're planning to take off with Sheeta. We've gotta hurry, or it'll be too late.

Dola: (Yelling, to boys) Come on! Boys stop eating!

Shalulu: (Ad-lib: Reaction, clearing out) Coming mama! Etc.

Lui: Okay, I'm going, Mama.

Pirate C: Ohh.

Pazu: Wait, are you gonna rescue Sheeta?

Anli: No you little squirt, we want her crystal.

Pazu: Wait a minute. You've got to have Sheeta to make the Aetherium crystal work, otherwise it's useless.

Pazu: (His back to camera) Dola please let me come with you. I need to save her.

Pazu: Sheeta means everything to me!

Dola: You know somethin'? You're acting like a snivelin' little crybaby.

Pazu: Maybe you're right, I should have protected Sheeta, but instead I was stupid and angry. But let me come with you and I swear I'll protect her this time.

Lui: (Sing-songy) Pazu loves Sheeta.

Dola: (To Lui) Be quiet!

Dola: (Contemplating) Hmm…

Dola: I guess you'd be useful in getting Sheeta to cooperate.

Dola: (Warning) You might never come back here again, Pazu.

Pazu: (Unflinched) I know.

Dola: Ready for what might happen?

Pazu: (Determined) Um-hm.

Dola: We leave here in one minute.

Pigeons: (Coo)

Pazu: (To pigeons, tenderly) Now you guys be good.

Dola: (To Pazu) Here, fasten this.

Pazu: Right!

Dola: (To her boys, shouting) Let's rendezvous at the tiger moth.

General: What a superb ship! [Moth not shown] Muska, has the girl surrendered the information?

Muska: It will take a little more time.

General: More time? Well you'll have plenty of that aboard *Goliath*. [MNS] We set out with her at first light.

Dola: Hurry, we have to get there before sun up.

Pazu: Sheeta.

Sheeta (as a little girl): [OS] (Crying)

[On] (Crying)

Grandma: Well well now, what shall we do?

Grandma: Sheeta, maybe grandma should teach you a spell. One that will help when you're in trouble.

Sheeta (As a little girl): A spell?

Grandma: Yes, my dearest. It is an ancient secret spell.

Grandma: Leetay Latuparita Ulus Aria Los Balu Netoreel.

Sheeta (As a little girl): (Trying to repeat after grandma) Leetay… ah—?

Grandma: (Gently explaining) The words mean, "Save me." "Save me and revive the eternal light." So Leetay Latuparita Ulus Aria Los Balu Netoreel.

Sheeta: (Whispers) Leetay Latuparita Ulus…Aria Los Balu Netoreel.

Sheeta: (Gasps & whimpers, reacting to crystal)

Sheeta: (Big reaction to crystal)

Muska: I knew it.

Muska: (Excited) It's the sacred light. The ancient documents were true. It's not just a legend.

Sheeta: (Confused and scared) What are you talking about?

Muska: (Off-On) (Pained) Aw!

Sheeta: (Reaction)

Muska: (Impatient, threatening) Tell me the spell. What are the secret words?

Guard A: Did you hear that?

Guard B: (Ah) Yeah, I did.

Guards A & B: (Ad-lib: Surprised and frightened walla—stay back, etc.) Huh?

Guard B: [Mouth not shown] Uh…

Guard B: (Panicking) I'm telling you this thing is alive!

Guard B: [OS] Alive! Do you hear me?! Alive!

Guards A & B: [On-Off] (Ad-lib: Startled and frightened walla and yell!)

Sheeta: (Gasps)

Muska: (Reaction)

Guard B: (In panic) Heeelp! It's alive. It's after us!! Arrgh!

Guard A: (Long shot) It's the robot! Run for your life!

Guard A: (Long Shot) It's come back to life!

Guard B: (Walla) Hurry, hurry! Sound the alarm. Quick Quick! There, there see? He's moving.

Muska: What's happening?

Sheeta: (Reaction to being dragged by Muska) Ah…ah. (Etc.)

Muska: It's coming toward us!

Officer #3: [On-Off] Shut the fire door. Hurry!

Soldiers: Uh?… (Fearful running walla)

Sheeta: Ah!

Muska: (Excited) The power!

Muska: Now I understand!

Sheeta: (Reacting to robot) Ah!…oh…(Continue reacting)

Muska: (His back to camera) It's that light!

Muska: The force of the sacred light has brought the robot back to life.

Muska: (His back to the camera) The way to Laputa has been opened!

Sheeta: Let me goooooo! (Continues reacting)

Muska & Sunglasses #2: Eh?… Uh… It's collapsing!

Sheeta: Aarrgh!

Muska & Sunglasses #1 & #2: (Reactions as they struggle)

Sheeta: (Ad-lib grunts as she scrambles to avoid falling)

Muska: It's going to fly!

Muska: (Screams)

Muska & Sunglasses #1 & #2: (Struggling)

Muska & Sunglasses #1 & #2: (Ad-lib: Running effort)

Sheeta: (Panicked breathing)

Sheeta: (Panting them yelps as she bumps into wall.)

Sheeta: (Scream and react)

Sheeta: (Cowering noises)

Sheeta: Oh!…Ah… (Starts to run)

Sheeta: (Panting and reacts)

Sheeta: Oh!…Ah!…

Sheeta: (In awe) It's Laputa!

Muska: At long last! I now know the way to Laputa!

Muska: Hurry, no time to waste.

General: (Upset) What do you mean? (Shouting angrily) I wanna know who's trying to blow up my fortress?

Soldiers: (Ad-lib: Walla, shouting orders to one another)

General: Are you there? Somebody answer me! Now!

Sunglasses #1: We're ready!

Sunglasses #2: (Calling out to Muska) You're connected now colonel.

Muska: This is colonel Muska. We have an emergency. You'll take your orders from me now.

Sheeta: (Slight gasp)

Muska: [OS] Fire on the robot the moment it appears, but do not hurt the girl! I repeat: Do not hurt the girl!

Sheeta: (Panic and reaction)

Soldiers: (Walla)

Officer #4: Hurry! I need that shell now!

Sheeta: (Reaction to beam of light—surprise)

Gunlayer: Fire!

Gunlayer: (Falling) Ah…Oh!?

Soldiers: (Cheering walla: We did it! Hurray! Etc.)

Officer #5: Up there now!

Soldier C: We demolished it!

Sergeant: Go get the girl. Over there.

Soldier A: [Mouth not shown] Is she dead?

Soldier C: [MNS] (To Sheeta) Hey, get up!

Sheeta: (Moans)

Soldier A: Nah, she's only fainted.

Soldier C: (To Sheeta) Come on!

Sergeant: (Reacting to robot head moving) Whoa?!

Soldiers: (Panic walla)

Muska: (Reaction to blast)

Soldiers: (Panic walla)

Soldiers: (Panic walla)

Anli, Shalulu, Lui: [MNS] (Yelps, yahoos, etc.)

Pazu: (Reacting to distant explosion) Whoa!

Dola: Must be some kind of war going on!

Pazu: Take her down, Dola!

Dola: Call me captain!

Dola: Just keep your big head down, Shalulu!

Sheeta: (Gasp! Shocked by what she sees)

Sheeta: (Gasps)

Sheeta: (To robot) Stop it! You're destroying everything.

Sheeta: (Her back to camera) Please stop.

Townsfolk: (Panic walla)

Lui: Captain mother, *Goliath* is moving.

Dola: If we stay on this heading, we'll be in the line of fire. Change course.

Pazu: Look, there she is! It's Sheeta!

Dola: What?!

Dola: Where did you see her?

Pazu: Steady as she goes, captain.

Pazu: [OS] She's on top of that tower!

Dola: One for all and all for mom! Cover me!

Pazu: [On-Off] (Calling out) Sheeta!

Sheeta: (Gasps as she sees Pazu)

Pazu: My hand! Take it!

Sheeta: Pazu!

Pazu: We've got to get a it a little closer Dola!

Dola & Pazu: [On-Off] (Reacting to flaptor's loss of balance) Ugh!

Pazu: Uhh!

Sheeta: (Desperately calling out) Pazu!

Sheeta: (Screams) Ah! [MNS] (To robot) But they're here to help me. Please, put me down!

Sheeta: [MNS] (Screams, reacting to explosion) No!!

Pazu: (Reacting to Dola falling back on him) Whoa!

(Desperately calling out) Sheeta!

Dola: (Passing out) Ugh.

Pazu: [OS] Dola!

Sheeta: No. They're falling.

Sheeta: (Whimpers as robot falls) (Desperately calling out) Help!

Pazu: (On-Off-On-Off) (Ad-lib straining & grunts) As he tries to get from behind Dola and pull control stick with all his might)

Pazu: (Talking to flaptor, tense) Ah, come on, pull up!

Pazu: (Shoved) Ugh!

Dola: (Completely back in control) It's now or never, Pazu. I'll take us in and you grab her!

Pazu: Right!

Sheeta: Over here!

Pazu: Okay, captain.

Dola: Now!

Muska: What are you doing? Fools! Don't let her escape!

Sunglasses #1: (Efforting)

Pazu: [On-Off] Jump!

Sheeta: (Jumping) Ah!

Sunglasses #1: (Efforting)

Muska: (Frustrated) An entire army and they're getting away?!

Muska: It's not over.

General: (Panting) Muska! Muska! What on earth happened to the robot?

Muska: (Calmly) We destroyed it. And the girl's gone.

General: What?! Ohh! Look at this, it's a disaster.

General: (Fuming) Aargh! (To the soldiers, barking) Ah, don't just stand there, men! Extinguish the fire. Organize a pursuit team!

Muska: Hm.

Muska: (In awe) It still possesses it's sacred light—

Muska: (Pointing to Laputa) (To his men) You may now go tell the general for me. We will be departing on time.

Sheeta: (Sobbing uncontrollably)

Lui: (Concerned) Sheeta? You okay?

Shalulu: (Mouth obscured by beard) (Serious, just between brothers) If I did something wrong, I'd really like to apologize for it Sheeta.

Dola: [OS] We all did something wrong, wasting our time on these two kids.

Dola: Here's your valley up ahead. I'll drop you off there and that'll be that.

Pazu: (To Sheeta, gently urging her) It's all right.

Pazu: Dola will you let us sail with you and the boys?

Dola: Call me "captain" darn it! And I don't see what the heck's in it for me since you lost the Aetherium crystal.

Pazu: We can work!

Sheeta: (Sincerely) And I have to find out the real truth about Laputa for myself, captain.

Dola: So you're not interested in money, but you want to find out the truth about Laputa.

Dola: (Smiling) Well I guess there's worse reasons for you wantin' to become a pirate.

Lui: (Expectant) Mother, I say let 'em come along.

Dola: (To Pazu and Sheeta) Toe the line and work hard or overboard you go.

Pazu: (Delighted) Yes, Captain!

Lui: (Exhilarated) Yess! No more swabbing the decks. Hooray!

Anli: I won't have to wash the dishes!

Shalulu: I've peeled my last potato. Yahoo!

Anli: [Mouth not shown] Whoopee!

Lui: [MNS] Woooweee!

Shalulu: (Calling out to Sheeta) Can you make pudding? I love pudding!

Lui: (Calling out) I get to lick the spatula!

Anli: (Calling out) And I like chocolate cake with that—oh, what's that frosting?—It's kinda pink and swirly and…

Dola: (to her boys) Will you shut up! Ah what can I tell ya, they just really like dessert.

Pazu & Sheeta: (As fighter docks) Whoa/ugh!

Dola: (To Pazu and Sheeta) And disembark!

Pazu: (Grunts as he steps off)

Sheeta: (Grunts as she steps off) [MNS] Whoa. Ah.

Pazu: (Reacting to almost stepping through cloth floor) Whoa, what is this ship made out of…cloth?

Dola: And don't you rip it!

Pazu & Sheeta: (Reacting to second fighter coming in) Ah?!

Lui: Come on, we'll go topside.

Sheeta: Whoa!

Dola: You're going the wrong way. Come here.

Sheeta: Ah…

Dola: [mouth not shown] (grumbling) I don't like slowpokes.

Lui: (To Pazu) You come this way.

Pazu: Whoa! (Time code off Lui)

Sheeta: Pazu?!

Dola: Come on, matey. I haven't got all day.

Lui: [Off-On] (Very aloof) Work, work, busy, busy, busy, left, right, left, right. You're not here to have fun.

Pazu: Whoa, this engine room is really amazing.

Lui: Is that what it's called? (Then yelling) Hey poppa, where are you!

Pazu: (Surprised) Ah!

Lui: (yelling) Hey pop! I finally found ya an assistant.

Poppa: Step yelling at me! – I [OS] can hear you. Believe me, sometimes I wish I couldn't.

Lui: (Sotto to Pazu) Ah hurry up. He's even tougher than my mother.

Poppa: (Straining a bit) It's too narrow. I can't reach.

Pazu: It's okay. I've got it.

Poppa: What's your name?

Pazu: (Telling his name to Poppa) Pazu.

Dola: But the beam from the crystal was pointing directly due east? You sure about this?

Sheeta: (Calmly explaining) Yes I'm sure. I could see the sun rising from the tower. You know, it's the end of grass-cutting season so—

Sheeta: —the sun rose not from due east, but a little further south. The light was pointing to the left of the hill from which the sun rose. (Turns to Dola) [MNS] You see?

Dola: (Interrupting, impressed/pleased) Pretty smart! (To Pirate B) Found anything yet?

Pirate B (Patch): Haven't found a single thing, captain.

Dola: [OS] They're jamming the airwaves to keep us from finding them. The sly devils.

Anli: Mom, how can we catch them when they're faster than we are?

Dola: Well, it looks like we're cruising on the windward side of 'em. So if we manage to ride the trade wind—

Dola: (Calculating with abacus) Let's see, according to my calculations—

Dola: (Mumbling to herself) — with wind velocity at ten…

Dola: (Bright) Looks to me like we'll catch 'em!

Dola: Attention all hands, now hear this!

Dola: [OS] (Through communication tube) *Goliath* is already under way for Laputa. We're going to set sail and go after 'em.

Dola: If we can catch the wind, we'll be on their heels by tomorrow.

Dola: [OS] (Through communication tube) Now the first man to spy *Goliath* will receive ten gold coins!

Shalulu: (Impressed) That's good money!

Dola: And, if the stories we've heard about Laputa are true, there will be enough treasure to make an honest pirate of us all.

Dola: All right. All hands aboard, look alive and get to work!

Poppa: Let 'er rip!

Dola: Course 98 degrees, velocity: 50.

Dola: (Her back to camera) Now you gotta start dressin' like a real pirate. Let's see here.

Lui & Pirate E: (Straining as they turn the wheel)

Sheeta: [MNS] (Ad-libs—rights/ah-ha's etc.)

Dola: And this is where you'll be working.

Lui: (Under his breath, admiring Sheeta) (Lovelorn sigh) Gulp.

Dola: [OS] This is the galley. I want it shipshape, sparkling clean and ready for action in one hour. That's an order!

Sheeta: [OS] (Stunned/daunted) Ah…

Dola: The boys get awful hungry, so you'll serve five meals a day. (As she opens door) Whaa?

Lui, Shalulu, Pirate C Pirate D, Pirate E: (Ad-lib: Whoa!...Etc. as they fall inside)

Sheeta: (Startled gasp)

Dola: Hmmm.

Lui & Shalulu: (Sheepish chuckle)

Lui, Shalulu, Pirate C Pirate D, Pirate E: (Smiles) Tootaloo!! Go, go!

Dola: (Yelling) You blubber heads. I'm not running a luxury cruise! Now get to work!

Sheeta: (Sighs) (Grunts with determination)

Sheeta: [OS] Come in.

Sheeta: I'll need some more time. Nothing's really ready yet. It took me a long time to clean everything up.

Lui: (Clears throat)

Sheeta: Ah yes? What is it?

Lui: (Under his breath) Duh.

Sheeta: Yes?

Lui: Er, I've finished my work for the moment and I've come to offer you my help.

Sheeta: [MNS] Well that's very kind of you… [On] Would you please hand me those plates over there?

Lui: With pleasure, my little an— (Discovering his brother already there)—gel.

Lui: (To his brother, reproachfully) [OS] What are you doing here? [On] I thought you said you had a stomachache.

Shalulu: (Cheerfully) I'm in love with you.

(Seeing Lui) ugh…

Lui: You!

Shalulu: …Hello.

Shalulu: (To his brother) Move!

Pirate C: (grumbling) It's too crowded.

Pirate D: [Mouth not shown] (Grumbling)

Anli: (Cheerfully) Hi, is there anything I can do? (Reacting to the boys) Ah? You!

Sheeta: Huh?

Shalulu, Lui, Pirate C. Pirate D: (Groan)

Poppa: What's come over you, my dear? It's not like you to challenge a ship like *Goliath*…you know the odds are against you.

Dola: I'm after treasure, that's all.

Poppa: (Chuckles knowingly, then) I must admit those kids are cute.

Dola: What do you mean by that, you old fool?

Poppa: Nothing. But that little girl does remind me of you not so long ago.

Dola: Who asked ya!?

Poppa: Nobody. Oh look, checkmate.

Dola: Hmm?

Pazu: (Walla, eating like pigs)
Lui: (Burps)
Shalulu, Anli, Pirate A, Pirate B, Pirate C, Pirate D, Pirate E: Fabulous!

Sheeta: Ah um, does anyone want more?

Pirate E: [MNS] More!

Sheeta: Yes? Oh?

Shalulu, Anli, Pirate A, Pirate B, Pirate C, Pirate D, Pirate E: More, more, more, more!

Two pirates: (Snoring)

Pazu: (Off-On) (Snoring)

Lui: [OS] Come on young pup.

Pazu: (Waking up) Um…hm?

Lui: Time to go on duty. It's cold, take this.

Sheeta: (Waking up noises then) Huh?

Dola: (Snoring)

Pazu: [MNS] I'll take over.

Anli: Thank you!

Pazu: (Reacting to Sheeta climbing up) Huh?

Pazu: (Surprised) Sheeta!

Sheeta & Pazu: (Ad-lib grunts, etc. as Pazu helps Sheeta into crow's nest and Sheeta almost blows away)

Sheeta: Wow! That was exciting!

Sheeta: (Delighted, in awe) Wow, you can see forever!

Sheeta: (Shivering) Brr…

Pazu: (Gently) Sheeta.

Sheeta: Huh?

Pazu: Here.

Pazu: [OS] (Through communication tube) (Gently talking to Sheeta) You okay?

Sheeta: [OS] (Through communication tube) Mmm, that's better.

Pazu: This is great. Now we can keep watch together.

Sheeta: [MNS] Pazu?

Pazu: Hm?

Sheeta: I'm really scared.

Sheeta: [OS] (Through communication tube) To tell you the truth, I don't want to go to Laputa.

Pazu: [OS] (Through communication tube) What do you mean? Didn't you tell Dola the truth?

Sheeta: [OS] (Through communication tube) No. I didn't lie to Dola. What I said about the light's direction is true, but…what if someone else dies?

Pazu: [OS](Through communication tube) You mean like the robot?

Sheeta: [OS] (Through communication tube) He died to save my life. I feel awful. All this is because of a spell my grandmother taught me and she taught me all sorts of spells. A spell to use when you're looking for something, a spell to cure sickness. There's even one she told me I must never use.

Pazu: [OS] (Through communication tube) What kind of spell?

Sheeta: [OS] (Through communication tube) The spell of destruction. She said that to give

power to good spells, I had to know evil ones too. But she told me never to use them.

Sheeta: (Mouth obscured by blanket) I was so scared when I learned that spell, I couldn't sleep. I didn't know the spells were connected to my necklace.

Sheeta: Uncle Pom was right when he said that it was dangerous for us to misuse the power of the crystal.

Sheeta: [OS] (Through communication tube) And what if Laputa has some power that can be used for great evil?

Sheeta: (Mouth obscured by blanket) I wish I'd thrown the crystal away.

Pazu: But then we never would have met. And anyway, even if you had, Laputa would still exist. Airplanes and flying machines are getting better and better. You know eventually some explorer or another is going to come across the city of Laputa one day and claim it.

Pazu: [OS] (Through communication tube) I can't really say I know what's best, but if Laputa really has such great power, we can't let it fall into the hands of bad people like Muska.

Pazu: (OS inside blanket) And—

Pazu: (Getting out of the blanket) Uh…If we run away now, Muska is gonna chase us forever.

Sheeta: But Pazu, I don't want you to become a pirate because of me.

Pazu: (Smiling) Ah. I'm not gonna become a pirate.

Pazu: [OS](Through communication tube) And don't worry, Dola will understand. She's much nicer than she pretends to be.

Pazu: And when we've finally found it, I promise you we'll go back to Gondoa.

Pazu: (His back to camera, but mouth movement partially visible) I want to see it all, Sheeta. The old house where you were born, the valley and everything.

Sheeta: [OS](Through communication tube) Oh, Pazu.

Pazu: [OS](Through communication tube) (Alarmed) Sheeta, what's that?!

Pazu: Right there! Under the ship. You see it?

Pazu: Captain, it's *Goliath* right under our bow!

Dola: (Shouting) Starboard rudder! Full speed ahead!

General: (Upset) Why don't you go after them. Muska?! Get them!

Muska: (Coldly) It's useless to look for them in the cloud cover.

General: (Upset) Hm?!

Muska: I don't need to waste my energy on a wild goose chase.

Muska: [OS] Besides, we're running right on schedule.

Dola: It's farther north than I figured. Pazu, listen carefully to me.

Dola: [OS](Through communication tube) Everything will be ruined if we lose track of *Goliath*. You've got good eyes, so I want you to watch her and keep us on course.

Pazu: How do I do that, captain?

Dola: The crow's nest can be made into a kite. See the metal handle on the bulkhead?

Pazu: I got it!

Dola: [OS](Through communication tube) Turn it clockwise!

Pazu: (Grunts as he turns the handle)

Dola: [OS](Through communication tube) Hook it up and then turn the handle. That will make the wings open.

Pazu: (Efforting)

Sheeta: (Efforting)

Sheeta: (Effort)

Dola: [OS](Through communication tube) Now extend the wire. You'll have to get the hang of flying it on your own!

Dola: Are you up there, Sheeta, my dear?

Sheeta: [OS] (Through communication tube) Yes.

Dola: Best you come down, right now!

Sheeta: [OS] Through communication tube) Why?

Dola: 'Cause you're a girl, a female. That's man's work!

Sheeta: But you're a female captain! I grew up in the mountains, I can do this!

Pazu: Sheeta, no!

Sheeta: (To Pazu) Be quiet. (To Dola) And Pazu agrees with me.

Dola: (Laughs, then) All rright me hearty. Once you take off you'll have to use the phone to communicate.

Sheeta: [OS] (Through phone) You mean this phone?

Lui: (Genuinely impressed) She is good.

Pazu: Right. I think we're set. Ready for takeoff.

Dola: [OS] (Through phone) Aye aye—anchors aweigh!

Sheeta: I don't see them.

Pazu: I think they must be hiding under the cloud cover.

Dola: [OS] (Through phone) Perhaps, but they could also be above you. Keep your eyes peeled.

Pazu: Roger! (Then reacting to sudden gust of wind) Whoa!! [Ends off]

Sheeta: Aw! [Ends off]

Pazu: Hang on tight!

Sheeta: [MNS] Ah-hm. Wha…

Sheeta: (Expelling of breath) Wha.

Pazu: (Struggling)

Dola: [OS] (through phone) What happened?!

Pazu: [OS] (through phone) Nothing. Just a gust of wind.

Pazu: [MNS] Didn't bother us at all. We're fine.

Pazu: We'll keep on watching.

Pazu: (To Sheeta) Afraid?

Sheeta: (Trying to be brave) Ah-uh.

Pazu: I've got the hang of this thing now. (Looking forward) Storm ahead!

Pazu: Sheeta. Look in my bag. There should be some rope in there.

Sheeta: Okay.

Pazu: Let's tie ourselves together. This storm is gonna be rough.

Sheeta: Good idea.

Lui: The mercury is dropping really fast, mom.

Dola: Blast our luck, boys. What a rotten time for a storm. When is sunup?

Shalulu: In one hour.

Pazu: Wait a minute. Something's not right.

Sheeta: The sun is coming up in the wrong place. We're out of position.

Pazu: You're right. We're supposed to be heading east and not north. We're going the wrong way. (To Dola OS) Captain!

Dola: Huh?! What d'ya mean we're headed north?

Shalulu: (Puzzled) But the compass needle is pointing east, mom.

Dola: There's something confusing the compass and I want to know what it is.

Sheeta: [OS] (Through phone) (Alarmed) there it is. Look!

Dola: There what is? Is it *Goliath*?!

Pazu: [OS] (Through phone) No, it's a cloud! But I've only seen one other like it.

Dola: (Puzzled) A cloud?

Sheeta: It's heading right for us.

Pazu: (gasp) That's it.

Dola: (Crescendoing shout) I'm not gonna captain my ship into the eye of a hurricane. Now pull back, pull back I tell ya! All engines reverse!

Pazu: We're being pulled into the center of the storm!

Dola: (Sincerely concerned—quickish) [OS] (Through phone) Sorry Pazu, we can't help you. You'll have to ride it out. Good luck, sailor!

Sheeta: (Screams)

Shalulu: I can't get it to turn!

Dola: Put more backbone into it, my boy!

Poppa: [OS] (Alarmed) Dola!

Poppa: Ah. The engine can't take it!

Dola: (Losing her temper) What do you want me to do about it? Just do what you can.

Dola: (Reacting) Clouds are breaking up.

Pazu: Look, it's the ocean.

Sheeta: (Gasps)

Dola: Pazu, it's a hurricane.

Pazu: I see it captain. We're going in!

Pazu: (Awed) Wow. It's just like dad said—two winds blowing in opposite directions!

Dola: Shiver me timbers. What a powerful storm.

Shalulu: [OS] (Whimpering) Mom, it's no use. We'll be sucked in!

Dola: If there's one thing I can't stand, it's a quitter!

Pazu: [OS](Through phone) Captain, Laputa's in there.

Dola: Laputa's where?!

Pazu: This is just the kind of storm my father saw and Laputa's in the middle of it.

Dola: [OS] It can't be. It would be smashed to pieces.

Sheeta: (OS-ON) (Alarmed) Pazu! Look there!

Pazu: (Indicating big trouble) Ah!

Dola: My boys, we have a dilemma, it's *Goliath* off the port bow.

Pazu: We're gonna go into the hurricane, Sheeta. My dad made it through alive and so will we.

Dola: Ready. Brace yourselves gentlemen—Ahhh!

Pazu: Ahh!

General: (His back to camera, pleased) They're hit! We did it! We got them!

Commander: (Urgent) If we don't turn we'll hit that storm.

Muska: (Calmly) All ahead full.

Commander: (Incredulous) Sir?

Muska: [OS] The light is pointing to the center of the whirlwind.

Muska: (Absolutely confident, calmly) Laputa is in that storm. We don't retreat, we go straight ahead. I'm positive we'll find it.

Pazu: Ready, Sheeta?

Sheeta: Yes!

Pazu: (Reacting to hallucination of his father) Ugh…huh?!

Pazu: (Moans, then awakening) Huh?! Ah?!...

Pazu: Sheeta! Hey! Are you all right? Wake up.

Sheeta: (Opening her eyes, smiling) Um…

Pazu: (Sotto) Look!

Sheeta: (Intake of breath)

Sheeta: (In awe) Laputa.

Sheeta: (Pulled up) Aw! (more reaction)

Pazu: Oh! I'm sorry. Here—oh… oh…

Sheeta: (Struggling to untie the knot) Ah…oh… Wait a minute!...uh…It's a very tight knot.

Sheeta: (Off-On) And my, my uhhh…my hands are trembling.

Sheeta: (lifted, surprised) Argh!

Pazu: (Whoops as he lifts Sheeta)

Pazu: [BTC] Wow!

Sheeta & Pazu: (Exhilarated laughter as they spin)

Pazu & Sheeta: (Ad-lib laughter and scream & grunts as they fall over and roll)

Pazu & Sheeta: [On-Off] (Giggling into big laughter)

Pazu: (Softly, pensive) Pretty birds.

Pazu: (Softly, pensive) Maybe their home is here.

Pazu: (Reacting to robot) Huh?

Pazu: I think he must be here to meet you, Sheeta.

Sheeta: (Nervous) But I don't have the Aetherium crystal.

Pazu: Wait…I've got to cut us loose. [Ends MNS]

Sheeta: (Flustered walla)

Pazu: [OS] Hey wait!

Pazu: (Alarmed) Don't touch that. You're gonna break that.

Sheeta: (To robot) Wait! Please mister robot, don't do that. We won't be able to go home without it.

Robot: Cling…Clang…Cluck

Sheeta: [OS] Look, Pazu.

Sheeta: It's a bird's nest. Ah…

Pazu: (Incredulous) That's why he's here.

Sheeta: I'm so happy the eggs are alright, Pazu.

Pazu: It must be his job to take care of them.

Robot: Cling, cluck.

Sheeta: He says to follow him.

Pazu: [MNS] How do you know?

Sheeta: [On-Off] (Overlaps with Pazu) I just know that's what he said.

Sheeta: Ahh…

Pazu: It's a city!

Pazu: Oh.

Pazu: I can't believe we're inside a building.

Pazu: (Reacting to bird outside) Huh?

Pazu: (Realizing with surprise) The walls are invisible.

Sheeta: Yeah.

Pazu: I wonder what happened here? This used to be a city of advanced technology.

Pazu: It must be monument. I wish we could read what it says.

Sheeta: Someone left some flowers, look.

Sheeta: (Turning to robot) Did you leave the flowers?

Sheeta: (Gasps as she realizes it's not the same robot, then) Huh?!

Pazu: Hey, that's a different robot!

Pazu: It looks like it's been frozen there forever.

Pazu: (Seeing other broken robots) Hey!

Pazu: They must have been protectors of the garden.

Pazu: And they've kept on guarding the place even long after all the people had gone.

Sheeta: (Turning) Huh?!

Sheeta: (To robot, moved) Oh… you've picked another flower for the grave. How kind of you.

Sheeta: (Gently, with emotion) Ah, thank you!

Pazu: He must be the only one left. It looks like all the other robots stopped working a long time ago.

Squirrels: (Squeaks off and on)

Robot: Cling, clang…

Pazu: (Delighted giggle)

Robot: Cling, clung, clung, cluck….

Pazu: [On-Off] You know what Sheeta, I bet he's not lonesome at all. He's got plenty of friends. The animals and the birds. He takes care of them.

Sheeta: (Small breath, moved, in tears)

Birds: Squawk squawk

Sheeta & Pazu: (Panting) (And as Sheeta stops) Oh!

Pazu: This way!

Sheeta: (Panting)

Soldiers: (Check sequence for walla)

Pazu: The army's destroyed this part of the city.

Sheeta: (Her back to camera) Oh, I sure hope Dola and the boys are alright.

Pazu: Me too. Where are they? Do you see them?

Pazu: [BTC] Wait! There they are!!

Pazu: They've got 'em prisoner.

Sheeta: (Gasp of horror)

Sheeta: [OS] They've been captured! We've got to help them.

Pazu: If we don't, they'll hang 'em from the yardarm!

Sheeta: Well, let's go!

Pazu: Come on, hurry!

Officer: [Mouth not shown] (As he runs) Sir! Sir!

Officer: We have managed to break down the wall general.

Officer: Just a sample of what we've found inside.

General: (Reacting to treasure) Oh!

General: (Reaction, impressed/ greedy excitement)

Officer: [OS] The city is full of treasure! Sir!

General: (To the pirates) Wouldn't you like to have this. I'm afraid I've got a different kind of necklace for you.

General: (To Muska) Have you radioed a report on Laputa's discovery, Muska?

Muska: (Cool) I was about to.

Soldiers: (Check walla through sequence)

General: See if you can make it difficult to decode.

General: (His back to camera, yelling to soldiers) Stop pocketing those jewels, you scum!

187

Muska: (His back to camera) The perfect thing to throw those fools off the scent.

Sheeta: We're up so high.

Pazu: I hope you're good at climbing trees, Sheeta.

Pazu: (Ad-lib grunts as she climbs down, then) I've got a plan.

Sheeta: (Ad-lib grunts as she climbs down)

Soldiers: (Check walla through sequence)

Pazu: (His BTC, disgusted) What a greedy pack of thieves.

Sheeta: We can't let them destroy the garden.

Pazu: (making a decision) We have to find the Aetherium crystal.

Sheeta: (Gasps)

Pazu: We have to find it! It's the only way we can protect the garden.

Pazu: (Explaining) I was wondering why all the storm clouds just disappeared.

Pazu: [OS] Then I realized if they hadn't cleared up, the army couldn't have made a landing.

Sheeta: (Realizing, fearful) Pazu, was it because of my spell?

Pazu: Well, I don't know for sure, but I think the power of the crystal disintegrated that storm.

Pazu: (His back to us) And now the castle has awakened from its sleep for whoever holds the crystal.

Pazu: We can't let Muska figure out how to use the crystal.

Pazu: If he does, it'll be the end of everything.

Sheeta: But even if we can get my grandmother's crystal back, how can we use its power?

Sheeta: (Gasps as an idea occurs to her, shocked) The spell, Pazu!

Pazu: The spell of destruction. Sheeta, it may be the only way!

Pazu: (Turning) (Gasp)

Soldiers: (Walla)

Pazu: (Sotto) We need to get down there.

Pazu & Sheeta: (Exertion/panting)

Pazu: I'll go first.

Sheeta: Right. Be careful.

Pazu: (Ad-lib grunts, etc. As he jumps, lands, loses his foothold and almost falls)

Sheeta: (Her back to camera, reacting to Pazu losing his foothold, stifling a scream) Ah!

Pazu: (Ad-lib grunts, etc. as he climbs, almost falls, etc.)

Sheeta: (Ad-lib stifled gasps of panic & whimpering, reacting to Pazu's action)

Muska: [OS] It's around here somewhere.

Sheeta: (Gasps, reacting to Muska's voice)

Muska: Hmm?

Pazu: (Straining)

Sheeta: (Stifled whimpering)

Pazu: (Straining as he pulls himself up)

Muska: [MNS] It should be here. (Turns)

Muska: (His back to camera) This is it!!

Sheeta: (React through shot)

Sunglasses #1: (Reacting to Pazu) Huh?!

Pazu: (Straining & struggling to climb up)

Sunglasses #1: (Shouting) It's the boy!

Sheeta: (Ad-lib grunts as she charges and knocks man over)

Sunglasses #1: (Relax to impact)

Pazu: (Calling out, alarmed) Sheeta!

Sunglasses #2: Stop!

Muska: (To his men, quickly) Don't shoot!

Sheeta: Aw!

Sheeta: [On-Off] (Ad-lib shrieking and struggling)

Muska: Well, well, looks like we've caught a little princess.

Pazu: (His back to camera) (Calling out desperately) Don't hurt her!

Pazu: (Bullet barely missing him) Ugh!

Sheeta: Pazu!

Soldier: (Pointing) Sir.

Soldier #1: [Off-On] (Calling out) It came from over here! Colonel what's happening down there?

Sheeta: (CM, OM, CM struggling)

Muska: We've found another pirate and there's one more hiding under your feet!

Soldier #1: [OS] Yes, sir! We'll get him!

Sheeta: (Struggling)

Pazu: (Calling out desperately) Sheeta, I'll find you!

Sheeta: (Calling out) Pazu!

Pazu: (Gasps reacting to the door disappearing)

Pazu: (Reacting to gunfire) Ugh!

Lui: Is that Pazu?

Dola, Lui, Shalulu, Anli, Poppa: (Reacting to poof! Surprised) Huh?

Lui: (As if to say, "what was that?") Ho. Hmm?

Shalulu: (As if to say, "Was it you who just farted, Dola?") Hmm?

Anli: (As if to say, "Aha, it was you!") Aha!

Dola: (Fretting) That wasn't me!

Dola: (Reacting to Pazu OS) Um…?

Soldier #2: I need the commanding officer.

Soldier #3: That way.

Soldiers: (Walla)

Soldier #2: General's waiting over there!

Officer: Guards! On the double now!

Pazu: [OS] Dola!

Dola: Huh?

Lui: (Surprised reaction)

Lui: (Reaction)

Pazu: Hi there. [OS] (Sotto) Sheeta's been captured. I'm going to save her. When I cut your ropes, make a run for it.

Dola, Shalulu, Anli, Lui: (Nonchalant humming)

Pazu: (Effort, cutting rope)

Pazu: Good luck now captain.

Dola: Wait a minute, boy!

Dola: [OS] You'd better take this.

Pazu: Huh? Uh, thank you!

Dola: (Pleased) The boy has become a man.

General: (OS) What?!

General: (Fuming) What do you mean Muska has destroyed all the radios?!

Hooded Soldier: (His back to camera) Sir. He must have done it while most of the men were outside.

Hooded Soldier: Several of the guards have been seriously injured.

Commissioned Officer B: We've spotted Muska heading for the black dome below sir!

Commissioned Officer B: [OS] He's not alone. He's got those other two men with him.

General: (Barking to his men) Now find him and arrest him!

Officer #1: All right! First platoon, move!

Commissioned Officer C: (His back to camera) Second platoon, fall in.

Commissioned Officer A: You are to shoot anyone who resists!

Commissioned Officer A: (His BTC) We must find colonel Muska now!

Sunglasses #1: Excuse me, colonel Muska, where are we?

Muska: We are in the center of Laputa, the castle above us means nothing!

Muska: (Extreme long shot) All of Laputa's scientific knowledge is contained in this chamber.

Muska: You may wait here, gentlemen.

Sunglasses #2: Colonel.

Sunglasses #1: Colonel, please!

Muska: This is a sacred place where only royalty is allowed to enter.

Muska: (Gasps then, cursing) What's happened here? Huh—err.

Muska: These filthy robots don't belong in this chamber.

Muska: Horrible things—I'll have them burned!

Muska: (On-Off, to Sheeta) This way. Come!

Muska: (Struggling to get rid of the roots) There it is!

Muska: [OS] This is it! [On] (Turns) See?

Sheeta: (Slight amazed gasp)

Muska: (His back to us) Uh!

Muska: Roots!

Muska: (His back to us) (Awed) At last, I have found it!

Muska: The largest aetherium crystal ever!

Muska: (His back to us) And the source of all the power in Laputa!

Muska: The amazing thing is this beautiful stone has been awaiting the return of its king for 700 years.

Sheeta: Seven hundred years?

Muska: Seven hundred years is a long time without a king, isn't it?

Muska: (Almost trembling with excitement) It's the black stone, just as the legend says!

Muska: (Waving away the bugs) Get away!

Muska: There it is, it's the same.

Sheeta: Who are you, Muska?

Muska: Yes, my dear, I too have an old secret name.

Muska: My real name is Romska Palo Ul Laputa.

Sheeta: (Gasps)

Muska: You and I have the same royal ancestors. We are both of noble blood.

Muska: [OS] But then, our ancestors left Laputa to live on earth. What a mistake.

Soldier #2: (His back to camera) (Amazed) The explosives have no effect.

Officer #4: (His back to camera) This is no ordinary stone.

General: Then use all of the dynamite we have!

Muska: [OS] (Echoed) (Cheerfully) General, there is no need to do that. You may come in.

General & Soldier #3, Officer #4: (Reacting to Muska's voice saying "general" surprised and alarmed) Huh?

General: Huh? Where are you Muska?

Sunglasses #1 & #2: (Long shot mouth not shown) (Scream as they fall)

General: (In panic) Ah? What?!

Soldiers #1, #2, # 3, #4 & officer: (On-Off-On) (Ad-lib panic walla: See action)

Pazu: (Reacting to jolt) Aw!

Pazu: (Screams as he falls on vine)

Pazu: (Grunts as he swings on vine, jumps to new vine and climbs—see action)

Pazu: (Noticing the porthole opening up) Huh?

Pazu: (Reacting to extending "feet" of Laputa)

General: (Three small sounds as he twitches his mouth three times)

Muska: [OS] (Echo) Really, I don't understand why you hesitate general. Please come in.

General: (Looking screen left) Blast him. (Looking screen right) All right. Follow me. (Running forward) Attaaaaack!

Officer or soldiers #1-4: (Walla: "Charge," etc.)

Pazu: (Dangling)

General: After him, men!

General: (Flustered) After him. Wait a minute. Hold on. Stop here. Wha wha, what is this, just where are you, Muska?

Muska: [OS] (Echoed) Please be quiet.

General: Huh?

Officer & Soldiers #1-4: (Fearful and surprised walla)

General: What's going on?

Muska: (Echoed) Hold your tongue, commoner. You are in the presence of the king of Laputa.

General: The man has gone crazy.

Muska: (Echoed) I thought I would show you an example of Laputa's power. We are about to celebrate the rebirth of the Laputian kingdom.

Pazu: (Surprised) Sheeta!

Muska: [OS] (Echoed) Prepare yourself for the thunder of Laputa.

Pazu: (Calling out) Sheeta! I'm coming! Uh…Ah..

Soldiers #1-4: [On-Off] (Reaction: "Whoa" etc.)

Pazu: (Reacting to explosion) Whoa (Struggling to hold on) Ugh…

189

Muska: (Echoed) The fire of heaven that destroyed Sodom and Gomorrah in the Old Testament.

Muska: [OS] (Echoed) The Rahmaniya referred to it as "Indra's Arrow."

Muska: (Echoed) The entire world will once again kneel before the power of Laputa.

General: I can only say well done, Muska. You're a credit to our country. As such, you deserve this reward.

General: Huh? Uh?

Muska: (Echoed) I have really had enough of your incredible stupidity.

Sheeta: (Gasps, then grunts as she smashes Muska's hand)

Sheeta: (Shouting) Run everyone! (Thrown aside) Aagh!

Muska: (Grunts, shoving Sheeta)

Muska: Goodbye!

General, Officer & Soldiers #1-4: (Panic walla and scream as they fall)

Commissioned Officers A & B, Soldiers #1-4: (Screaming as they flee)

Muska: [On-Off] (Triumphant laughter)

Soldiers: (Soldier walla) Check through end of sequence)

Dola: Blimey. More robots.

Lui: And there's a lot of 'em.

Dola: Make a run for it!

Dola: Check the flaptors!

Shalulu: Okay, mom. They're ready to travel.

Lui: [OS] It's time to go momma.

Dola: Hush up. They don't know we're here.

Dola: Tarnation, now where are Pazu and Sheeta? I can't leave without 'em.

Sheeta: (Slapped hard) Ugh!

Muska: You had better be gracious to the new king, dear.

Muska: (Grunts as he shoves Sheeta)

Sheeta: (Shoved, falling) Ow!

Muska: You and I will be spending quite a lot of time together.

Muska: [MNS] Look at the fools!

Muska: Unbelievably stupid.

Sheeta: (Struggling to free herself)

Muska: [OS] Pathetic. They simply don't understand it is useless to fight me.

Pazu: (His back to camera-on) (Ad-lib straining, clinging, gasping)

Pazu: (Blown by the explosion) Whooa!!

Pazu: (Landing in hole) Ugh!

Pazu: (Ad-lib straining, clinging)

Pazu: (Reacting to robot) Huh?

Pazu: (Long shot) Robots!

Robot: Cling clung….

Pazu: Uh? Whoooaaa!

Pazu: (Grunts as he gets back in the tube) [Mouth not shown]

Pazu: (Ad-lib effort & panting as he climbs up)

Pazu: (Calling out) Sheeta!

Sheeta: (Gasps, reacting to explosion)

Muska: [OS] A superior being such as myself has only one option…

Sheeta: (Shocked) Ah! (Turning away) Oh!

Muska: Burn them! (Turning to Sheeta) Don't you agree, Princess Lusheeta?

Muska: (Amused) Oh!

Muska: [MNS] Ha, ha, ha! Look! (Maniac laughter)

Muska: (Bitten by Sheeta) Argh! (Hitting her) You insolent little brat!

Sheeta: (Landing painful) Ugh!

Sheeta: (Ad-lib grunts as she gets up and takes off running)

Muska: (Growls angrily, then looking around) Sheeta!

Muska: Be a good girl and give the crystal back.

Sheeta: [Mouth not shown] (Out of breath) Please open up! Please! (Starts sobbing)

Sheeta: (As the door opens, falling forward) Ugh!

Sheeta: (Ad-lib whimpering grunts as she gets up and runs)

Muska: Sheeta, listen to me. Be reasonable. [On-Off] (Laughs, then) There's no way you can escape.

Sheeta: (Desperate) Please open! Help me!

Pazu: (Off-On) (Ad-lib grunts, panting, etc. as he loads and fires gun)

Pazu: (Ad-lib grunts & panting as he gets up, struggles through the hole and runs)

Pazu: Sheeta!

Sheeta: (Panting & swallowing hard)

Muska: (Gloating chuckles, enjoying the hunt) (Maniacal laughter)

Sheeta: (Trips and falls) Ugh!

Sheeta: (Ad-lib heavy panting as she stops)

Pazu: [OS] (Calling out) Sheeetaa!

Sheeta: (Recognizing the voice) Pazu!

Sheeta: Where are you?

Pazu: [OS] (Calling out) Sheeta! Over here. Sheeta!

Sheeta: Ah!

Pazu: [OS](Voice very close) Sheeta!

Sheeta: (Her back to camera) You're alive!

Pazu: (Through the crack) Stand back!

Pazu: I'm gonna blast through!

Pazu: Here we go!

Sheeta: [OS] No! Pazu!

Sheeta: Hurry, take this! Muska's coming! Hurry!

Pazu: [On-Off] (Ad-lib straining to reach for crystal)

Sheeta: [MNS] Here, take it.

Sheeta: Throw it into the ocean!

Pazu: (Finally taking the crystal in his hand) MM! [Mouth not shown]

Pazu: (Reaction to Muska's arrival)

Pazu: (Being fired at) Ugh!

Muska: (To Pazu) Better protect that crystal if you want to see the girl alive. Do you hear me?

Pazu: (Ad-lib grunts, etc., as he loads and fire gun, reloads and fires again)

Sheeta: [Off-MNS] (Scream, panicked running. React to shot)

Muska: Get up princess, the game is over!

Sheeta: (Exhale-Recoup)

Muska: How appropriate that we've ended up in the throne room! Now get over here.

Sheeta: (With quiet dignity and authority of a queen) This is no longer a throne room. This is a tomb for the both of us.

Sheeta: You see, a king without compassion does not deserve a kingdom. You will never possess the crystal.

Sheeta: [OS] You and I will die here together.

Sheeta: (Long shot) Now I understand why the people of Laputa vanished. There is a song from my home in the valley of Gondoa that explains everything. It says "Take root in the ground, live in harmony with the wind. Plant your seeds in the winter, and rejoice with the birds in the coming of spring."

Sheeta: No matter how many weapons you have, no matter how great your technology might be, the world cannot live without love.

Muska: Laputa will live. I will return it to life!

Muska: (His back to camera) Laputa's power is the dream of all mankind.

Muska: (His back to camera) Your ears are next—unless you get on your knees and obey me. I command you, give me that stone.

Pazu: [OS] (Screaming) Stop right there, Muska!

Pazu: I've hidden the stone. If you do anything to harm Sheeta, you'll never get it back!

Sheeta: No Pazu, run away before he kills you as well as me!

Muska: Pazu, look boy…give me the stone and the girl will live. Otherwise, I'll kill her!

Muska: [OS] Are you planning on fighting me? Go ahead, use that cannon you can hardly lift.

Pazu: You can have the stone if you let me talk to Sheeta.

Sheeta: No Pazu! Get out of here and throw the crystal away!

Muska: I'll give you one minute, starting now.

Sheeta: (distraught, almost collapsing into Pazu's arms) Ahh, Pazu!

Pazu: (Sotto, evenly) Sheeta listen to me very carefully. Whisper the spell to me.

Pazu: (Gently, reassuringly) I'll say it with you.

Sheeta: (Small gasp)

Pazu: Just put your hand in mine and trust me.

Pazu: Dola and the boys are free. Don't worry about them.

Sheeta: (Small breath, smiling)

Muska: Time's up! What's your answer?

Muska: Huh?!

Pazu & Sheeta: (Uttering the spell of destruction) Balus!!

Pazu & Sheeta: (Reaction to crystal's energy explosion)

Muska: (Reaction & scream)

Muska: (Pitiful groans) Ugh…! My eyes! I can't see!

Muska: (Pitiful groans)

Shalulu: We can't wait anymore mom.

Dola: All right then, let's shove off!

Anli: Hurry up!

Anli: Look at that, the whole thing's collapsing!

Lui: Poor kids, I'll really miss them. (Sniffs)

Dola: They used the spell of destruction. They saved Laputa from the evil hands of Muska.

Shalulu: (Sobbing, then) Hum?!

Pirate E: (Sobbing, then) Um?

Lui: Mother, look! What is that big blue light up there?

Pirate B: It's a big stone!

Dola: That tree is getting away with our treasure. Get it, get it! Move!

Dola: Come on! Move, you sacks of dead weight! Move, move!

Dola's Boys: (Reaction)

Lui: (Protesting) (Whoa) Now mother, let's not get cranky. Downshift!

Pazu: [OS] (Very gently) Sheeta.

Sheeta: (Softly) Pazu?

Pazu: (Long shot) It looks like these roots saved us.

Sheeta & Pazu: (Ad-lib: climbing effort)

Pazu: It looks fine. It should work.

Pazu: Ready?

Sheeta: Ready.

Pazu: (Grunts as he kicks off) Now.

Dola: What's going on here? It's getting away from us!

Dola: (Jiggling from vibration, frustrated) Why the deuce aren't we gainin' altitude?

Anli: (Jiggling) There's just too much weight to gain altitude—(His face is squashed) [OS] Ugh!

Dola: (Noticing kite) Huh?!

Dola: (Recognizing the kids) Oh!

Lui: (Excited) Sheeetaaaa!!

Lui: (Cheering walla)

Shalulu, Anli, Poppa, Pirates A-E: (Cheering walla)

Shalulu: She's alive!....Sheeta is alive!

Sheeta: (Her back to camera) Dola!

Dola: Thank goodness you're alive!

Pazu: So are you! This is great!

Poppa: No it's not. My poor little ship is gone forever…(weeps)

Dola: (To Poppa) Stop with the cryin' ya big baby. I'll get you another ship!

Dola: (To Sheeta) Poor little thing. There's nothing worse than having your pigtails shot off.

Sheeta: [MNS] What have you got under there?

Dola: Oh, my fault! You must have hurt yourself on these.

Dola: [OS] Now, how'd they get inside my blouse.

Lui, Shalulu, Anli, Poppa, Pirates A-E: (Ad-lib yeah! Etc.)

Shalulu: All good pirates listen to their mom!

Sheeta: Aha…(Laughs)

Pazu: (Bursts into laughter)

Shalulu: (Laughs)

Dola, Sheeta, Pazu, Shalulu, Anli, Poppa, Pirates A-E: (laughter)

The End

Credits

EXECUTIVE PRODUCER   Yasuyoshi Tokuma

ASSOCIATE EXECUTIVE PRODUCERS
Tatsumi Yamashita   Hideo Ogata

ORIGINAL STORY AND SCREENPLAY
Hayao Miyazaki
(Published by Tokuma Shoten as a series in *Animage* monthly magazine)

MUSIC   Joe Hisaishi

SONG   "Kimi wo nosete"
LYRICS: Hayao Miyazaki   MUSIC: Joe Hisaishi
PERFORMANCE: Azumi Inoue (Tokuma Japan)

SUPERVISING ANIMATOR   Tsukasa Tannai

LEADING KEY ANIMATOR   Yoshinori Kanada

KEY ANIMATION
Masako Shinohara	Michiyo Sakurai
Masaaki Endo	Noriko Moritomo
Makiko Futaki	Atsuko Otani
Kazuyuki Kobayashi	Tadashi Fukuda
Megumi Kagawa	Hirotsugu Kawasaki
Mahiro Maeda	Kitaro Kosaka
Shinji Otsuka	Yasuhiro Nakura
Toshio Kawaguchi	Osamu Nabejima
Katsuya Kondo	Toyoaki Emura
Kazuhide Tomonaga	

ANIMATION CHECK
Tadashi Ozawa   Yasuko Tachiki

INBETWEEN / CLEAN-UP ANIMATION
Kenji Kobayashi	Eiko Miyamoto
Eiichiro Hirata	Takashi Motomochi
Mika Sugai	Kyoko Nakano
Yoshie Takamine	Shinji Morohashi
Keiichiro Hattori	Kazuhisa Nagai
Takao Yoshino	Hiroomi Yamakawa
Toshiharu Murata	Machiko Araya
Yoshiya Shigebayash	Masako Sakano
Seiko Azuma	Komasa
Naoko Takeba	Masashi Kaneko
Wakako Ueda	Yuichi Katayama

SUPPORTING ANIMATION STUDIOS

Doga Kobo
Yoshimi Kanbara	Keisuke Makinoda
Tatsuji Narita	Kiyo Mizutani
Yasuko Suzuki	Yumi Kawachi
Masumi Ishiguro	Tazuko Fukudo
Yayoi Matsushita	Satoshi Ida

Studio Toto
Toshitaka Henmi	Sachiko Tsunoda
Shizuko Minami	Minoru Okamoto
Toru Morita	

Oh Production
Keiko Nagai	Yoshiko Kato
Tsutomu Awada	

Kusama Art
Yoshiko Sato	Akiko Yamaguchi
Satoshi Shigeta	

Shindo Production
Kyoko Higurashi	Akemi Seki
Ritsuko Tanaka	Naoyoshi Yamamuro
Hitoshi Ebara	

Studio Fantasia
Akiko Teshima	Sadao Takahashi
Kumiko Otani	Emiko Iwayanagi
Miyako Izumi	

Visual '80
Atsuko Narumi	Sumio Watanabe
Kuniko Hamano	

Studio Gallop
Mariko Araya	Kazumi Okabe
Toshiko Saito	

Studio Kuma
Hayato Teshima	Isao Hoshi

| ART DIRECTION | Toshiro Nozaki |
| | Nizo Yamamoto |

BACKGROUND

Mutsuo Koseki	Kazuhiro Kinoshita
Masaki Yoshizaki	Katsu Hisamura
Kumiko Iijima	Kiyomi Ota
Yamako Ishikawa (HARMONY TREATMENT)	
	Noriko Takaya

| SPECIAL EFFECTS | Go Abe |
| | Shinji Teraoka |

| COLOR DESIGN | Michiyo Yasuda |

| INK AND PAINT CHECK | Homi Ogiwara |

| INK AND PAINT | Chiharu Mizuma |
| | Noriko Ogawa |

Hiromi Nagamine	Emiko Ishii
Masako Nabeya	Yukiko Sakai
Kumi Shimada	Fumiya Sakamoto
Ryusuke Mita	Hiromi Nakada
Kazue Yanagisawa	Keiko Kihara
Mari Miyashita	Yoshiko Takasago

SUPPORTING INK AND PAINT STUDIOS

Studio Killy

Toshichika Iwakiri	Michiko Nishimaki
Yukie Naito	Taeko Sato
Fusako Takami	Masako Natsui
Shinichiro Kuze	Nobuko Nakada
Kanae Aoshima	Naomi Takahashi
Miyoko Nishiyama	Harumi Machii

Studio Fantasia

Tomohisa Iizuka	Rumiko Nagai
Tomoko Danjo	Yuko Kikuchi
Mariko Tanazawa	Toshiko Asano

Production Act

Hiroko Yokoyama	Yumiko Honda
Mieko Taguchi	Ayako Murano
Etsuko Shimoda	Yoshie Komatsu
Hiroyuki Kuraoka	Yoko Kazama

Studio Oz

Akihiko Isozaki	Hiroko Takashima
Naomi Masuda	Juki Shinoda
Akemi Hosoya	Keiko Hiraga

Group Joy

Asako Ohashi	Kumiko Suzuki
Akiko Sudo	Mikako Sodeyama
Yoshie Murakami	Shinnosuke Sato

Studio Hibari

Kenji Narita	Toshie Akiyama
Noriko Arakawa	Fumie Kato
Yoko Suzuki	

Studio Korumi

| Yukitaka Shishikai | Katsutoshi Yamagata |

CAMERA	Takahashi Production
	Hirokata Takahashi
	Takashi Shirakami

Takeo Kobayashi	Izumi Kasama
Yasuyoshi Toyonaga	Taizo Matsuzaki
Toshiyuki Fukushima	Yoshiaki Yasuhara
Takahisa Ishizuka	Hajime Noguchi
Yukio Miyajima	

| TITLES | Takagu Atelier |

| EDITING | Takeshi Seyama |
| | Yoshihiro Kasahara |

| AUDIO DIRECTOR | Shigeharu Shiba |

RECORDING AND SOUND MIXING

| | Shuji Inoue |

SOUND EFFECTS	E & M Planning Center
	Kazutoshi Sato
	Hironori Ono

ASSISTANTS TO THE DIRECTOR	
	Tsutomu Iida
	Satoshi Kimura
	Norihiko Suto

| PRODUCTION DESK | Naoyuki Oshikiri |

PRODUCTION ASSISTANTS	
	Naotake Furusato
	Hirokazu Kihara
	Toshitsugu Hara
	Masashi Atsumi
	Kaoru Muto

| ADVERTISING PRODUCER | |
| | Masaya Tokuyama |

| MUSIC PRODUCTION | Mitsunori Miura |
| | Tokuma Japan Co., Ltd. |

| AUDIO RECORDING | Omnibus Promotion |

| RECORDING STUDIO | Tokyo T.V. Center |

| FILM DEVELOPING | Imagica |

Tokuma Shoten "Tenku no shiro Laputa" PRODUCTION COMMITEE

Hiroyuki Kato	Toshio Suzuki
Akira Kaneko	Osamu Kameyama
Kazutoshi Takigawa	Minoru Tadokoro
Masahiro Kasuya	Tsutomu Otsuka
Takao Sasaki	Mikio Takeda
Mitsuru Menjo	Tomoko Kobayashi

| PUBLISITY SUPPORT | Dentsu Inc. |

| DISTRIBUTION | Toei Company, Ltd. |

| PRODUCTION | Studio Ghibli |
| | Toru Hara |

| PRODUCER | Isao Takahata |

| DIRECTOR | Hayao Miyazaki |

IMAGE SONG "Moshimo sora wo tobetara"
LYRICS Takashi Matsumoto
MUSIC Kyohei Tsutsumi
PERFORMANCE Yoko Kohata (Tokuma Japan)

VOICES

PAZU	Mayumi Tanaka
SHEETA	Keiko Yokozawa
DORA	Kotoe Hatsui
MUSKA	Minori Terada
UNCLE POM	Fujio Tokita
GENERAL	Ichiro Nagai
BOSS	Hiroshi Ito
BOSS'S WIFE	Machiko Washio
SHALULU	Takuzo Kamiyama
LUIS	Yoshito Yasuhara
ANLI	Sukekiyo Kameyama
OLD ENGINEER	Ryuji Kai
MADJI	Tarako

Eiken Mine	Reiko Suzuki
Takahiro Hirai	Tomomichi Nishimura
Shinya Otaki	Hideki Fukushi
Nobuyuki Furuta	Yoshitada Otsuka
Kazumi Tanaka	Masashi Sugawara
Toshihiko Seki	Megumi Hayashibara

Kimi wo Nosete (Carrying You)

Lyrics by Hayao Miyazaki
Composed & Arranged by Joe Hisaishi
Vocal Performance by Azumi Inoue

あの地平線　輝くのは	Out beyond the setting sun, and hidden from your eyes
どこかに君をかくしているから	Holding you apart from me. Dancing across the skies.
たくさんの灯がなつかしいのは	When the heavens fill with stars, in purple scented night
あのどれかひとつに、君がいるから	I know that you are one of them, shimmering beads of light.
さあ　でかけよう　ひときれのパン	Shall we pack the things we have, and go off just we two
ナイフ、ランプ　かばんにつめこんで	Bread, a candle and a knife, just to see us through.
父さんが残した　熱い想い	My father's dreams still burning in my heart
母さんがくれた　あのまなざし	My mother's eyes ever smiling songs of love
地球はまわる　君をかくして	The earth turns round and round, taking you away from me
輝く瞳　きらめく灯	Blinking, twinkling points of light, shining in the sky.
地球はまわる　君をのせて	The earth turns round and round, taking you away from me
いつかきっと出会う　ぼくらをのせて	When will it swing back again, carrying you to me.
父さんが残した　熱い想い	My father's dreams still burning in my heart
母さんがくれた　あのまなざし	My mother's eyes ever smiling songs of love
地球はまわる　君をかくして	The earth turns round and round, taking you away from me
輝く瞳　きらめく灯	Blinking, twinkling points of light, shining in the sky.
地球はまわる　君をのせて	The earth turns round and round, taking you away from me
いつかきっと出会う　ぼくらをのせて	When will it swing back again, carrying you to me.

THE ART OF
CASTLE
IN THE SKY

Based on a Studio Ghibli Film
by Hayao Miyazaki

English Adaptation/Jocelyne Allen
Design & Layout/Izumi Evers
Copy Editor/Justin Hoeger
Editor/Nick Mamatas

Tenku no Shiro Laputa
(Castle in the Sky)
Copyright © 1986 Studio Ghibli

© 1986 Studio Ghibli
First published in Japan
by Tokuma Shoten Co., Ltd.

Printed in China

Published by VIZ Media, LLC
P.O. Box 77010
San Francisco, CA 94107

First printing, October 2016
Third printing, January 2024

viz.com